the complete
triathlete's
training manual

the complete
triathlete's
training manual

OLIVER ROBERTS

BARRON'S

This edition for the United States, its territories and dependencies, and Canada published in 2010 by Barron's Educational Series, Inc.

Conceived and created by
Axis Publishing Limited
8c Accommodation Road
London NW11 8ED
www.axispublishing.co.uk

Creative Director: Siân Keogh
Designer: Sean Keogh
Project Editor: Anna Southgate
Production Manager: Bili Books

NOTE
The opinions and advice expressed in this book are intended as a guide only. The publisher and author accept no responsibility for any injury or loss sustained as a result of using this book.

All inquiries should be addressed to:
Barron's Educational Series, Inc.
250 Wireless Blvd.
Hauppauge, NY 11788
www.barronseduc.com

Library of Congress Control Number:
2009924057

ISBN-13: 978-0-7641-4384-7
ISBN-10: 0-7641-4384-0

Printed in China
9 8 7 6 5 4 3 2 1

contents

introduction

I can still remember my first triathlon. I remember swimming with my face out of the water. I remember the thrill of passing someone during the bike ride. I remember my inner glee as I rode by. I remember running, exhausted, through the finish line and staggering across the field to a table of postrace treats—cherries from a local orchard and cups of orange juice. But most of all I remember how much fun it was, how completely hooked I was, and how I couldn't wait until I could do it all again.

Why tri? The fun

Swim, bike, run. It doesn't sound like much, but there's something about triathlon that's addictive. Maybe it's that training for three sports will give you a more interesting routine than training for one alone. Maybe it's the satisfaction you'll get from crossing the finish line having achieved your goal, whether it's a time, a win, or simply to finish. Maybe it's the many fun and, often, amazing people you'll meet along the way. The only way to really understand is to get out there and join in.

Why tri? The fitness

Regular exercise can help you achieve and maintain a healthy weight, reduce your risk of illnesses such as cancer, heart disease, and Alzheimer's, and increase your strength. Triathlon's unique mix of high- and low-impact sports will even help improve your balance and bone strength.

Why tri? The flash

It may sound shallow, but one of the really cool things about triathlon is the kit. Funky running shoes, carbon bicycles with disc wheels, cool shades—triathletes are often on the cutting edge of cool. This may sound like showing off, but it's actually a sign of an openness to new things that extends to the way they welcome newcomers to their sport.

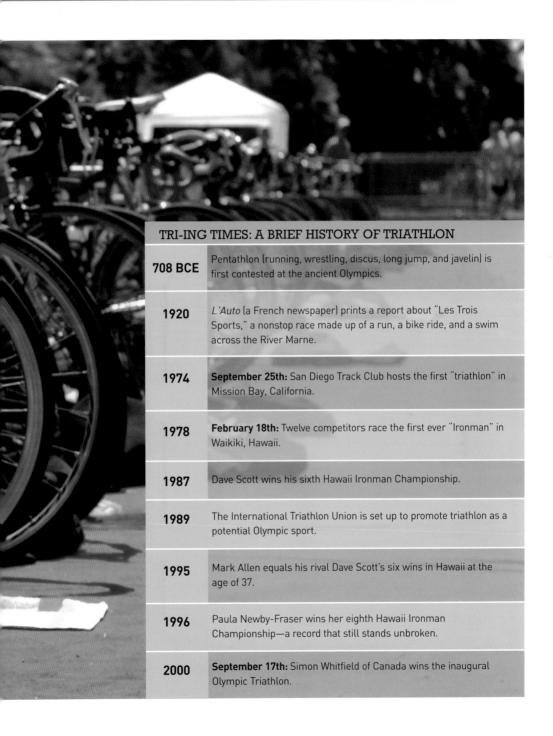

TRI-ING TIMES: A BRIEF HISTORY OF TRIATHLON

708 BCE	Pentathlon (running, wrestling, discus, long jump, and javelin) is first contested at the ancient Olympics.
1920	*L'Auto* (a French newspaper) prints a report about "Les Trois Sports," a nonstop race made up of a run, a bike ride, and a swim across the River Marne.
1974	**September 25th:** San Diego Track Club hosts the first "triathlon" in Mission Bay, California.
1978	**February 18th:** Twelve competitors race the first ever "Ironman" in Waikiki, Hawaii.
1987	Dave Scott wins his sixth Hawaii Ironman Championship.
1989	The International Triathlon Union is set up to promote triathlon as a potential Olympic sport.
1995	Mark Allen equals his rival Dave Scott's six wins in Hawaii at the age of 37.
1996	Paula Newby-Fraser wins her eighth Hawaii Ironman Championship—a record that still stands unbroken.
2000	**September 17th:** Simon Whitfield of Canada wins the inaugural Olympic Triathlon.

getting started

Swim. Bike. Run. When you break it down, triathlon isn't nearly as complicated as it can sometimes seem. The first chapter of this book does exactly the same thing. Over the next few pages, we'll take the concept of a triathlon and split it up. We'll look at each discipline in turn, and explain the training you'll need to do, how the races work, and what you'll need to do to get started on the road to competing in your first triathlon, or completing your fastest triathlon.

how to use this book

Under starters orders

If triathlon has a flaw (and we'd say that it's only a teeny tiny one), it's that there can seem like a lot to take on board when you're just starting out. This book is especially designed to help ease that process.

How to use this book

We've tried really hard to cover all the bases in this book. Chapter 1 gives you an overview of the sport, the different distances you can race, how fit (or not) you need to be, and what's involved in each of three disciplines—in terms of both training and racing. Chapter 2 looks at clothes and equipment. It suggests some basic kit essentials and gives you tips on features to look for to get the most for your money. You'll also find advice about choosing the right bike, finding which running shoes you need, and learning how a wetsuit should fit. Chapter 3 deals with diet, first laying out the principles of eating for a fitter, healthier you, and then looking at what you should eat (and drink) before, during, and after different training sessions. Chapter 4 focuses on the heart of triathlon—training. Here you'll find some golden rules for successful training, and advice on how to measure and monitor your efforts whether you're swimming, cycling, or running. You'll also find suggestions on how to keep yourself injury- and illness-free with a mixture of basic advice and treatment techniques, simple core stability exercises, and a few of our favorite postworkout stretches.

Training schedules

Chapter 5 is your secret weapon—a series of six, carefully created training schedules. You'll find schedules aimed at all the main triathlon distances—even Ironman—that you can either drop into at the level that's right for you, or work through as you gradually get fitter and set your racing sights ever higher. You'll even find a training diary in which you can log your progress.

THE TRAINING SCHEDULES

1 **STARTER LEVEL**
Starting from nothing? This plan will take you from zero to novice or sprint-race hero in just six sessions a week.

2 **STARTER LEVEL**
Starting from nothing? This plan will take you from zero to novice or sprint-race hero in just six sessions a week.

3 **INTERMEDIATE LEVEL**
Feel the need for speed? This sprint-racing masterplan is just what you need.

4 **INTERMEDIATE LEVEL**
If you've tried one Olympic-distance race, but are sure you can do better, this plan will help you succeed in just twelve weeks.

5 **EXPERT LEVEL**
Take your fitness to a new level with this 16-week, half-Ironman training plan.

6 **EXPERT LEVEL**
A carefully constructed, 24-week training schedule for tackling your first Ironman.

get set

One of the great things about triathlon is that it's a fitness activity with a built-in goal—your target race. You get runners who simply run, cyclists who simply cycle, but triathlon is about preparing for an event. This makes motivation easier, it gives structure to your training, and it encourages you to keep raising your game as you get ever fitter and faster. Triathlon races fall into six broad categories.

Novice

This is where most triathletes start racing. The distances are short, and the course is often closed to traffic. In some cases, you'll only be able to enter one or two sprint races, after which you'll be expected to move "up" to supersprints and sprints.

Supersprint

If swimming isn't your strong point, the supersprint may be your chance to shine. Really just a sprint-distance race with a shorter swim (usually 400 m), and sometimes a shorter bike and run, these races are often based around swimming pools.

Sprint
750 M SWIM/20 KM BIKE/5 KM RUN

Traditionally half the length of a standard-distance race (see below), sprint races offer an exciting mix of speed and endurance. The fastest in the field will finish these races well inside an hour, and race them most weekends over the summer.

NO EXCUSES!

Don't let little fears stop you taking up triathlon

I'm too old: Men and women have been finishing triathlons, up to Ironman and beyond, into their 70s and 80s. You're not too old. Regular training has even been shown to slow down the effects of aging and help prevent age-related illnesses.

I'm too slow: Triathlons are first and foremost about racing yourself—indeed, it's one of the few sports that has a series of age-group-based national and world championships. Watch a race and you'll see many different sizes, shapes, and speeds of people taking part. You are not too slow.

I'm too fat: Whatever your weight, you can always try to change it. In fact, triathlon's combination of low- and high-impact activities, and its emphases on consistent training and "racing yourself" can be the ideal way to shed those unwanted pounds.

I'm too busy: Triathlon training does take time, certainly, but not as much time as you might think. And you'll be surprised how easy it is to fit things in, particularly if you get a partner or family member involved as well.

Short course
1500 M SWIM/40 KM BIKE/10 KM RUN

Also known as an "Olympic-distance race" in honor of its addition to the games in 2000, this is the classic 2–3 hour triathlon that you'll see taking place in major cities. The swim for a standard distance will often be a "mass start" in open water (see page 15), so you need to be confident swimming without lanes.

Middle distance
1.2 MILE SWIM/56 MILE BIKE/13.1 MILE RUN

Okay, it's not in the middle, but the jump between standard and the top is so huge that these races have emerged to bridge the gap. Also called a half-Ironman (for all the obvious reasons), this race has

HEALTH CHECK

However fit you think you are, you should always get your doctor to give you a general checkup before you start working toward your first triathlon.

become increasingly popular since the start of the well-financed 70.3 series in 2005.

Long distance
2.4 MILE SWIM/112 MILE BIKE/26.2 MILE RUN

The classic long-distance triathlon is the Ironman Series (though there are others), the world championships of which are held every year on Kona, Hawaii. Mentally and physically demanding, both in training and racing, this is triathlon unbound.

Do you have a heart condition?

Does your family have a history of heart disease?

Have you ever been told that you should only do physical exercise recommended by a doctor?

Do you feel chest pain when physically active?

Have you ever had chest pains when not active?

Do you ever lose balance due to dizziness?

Do you have a bone or joint problem?

Are you taking drugs for blood pressure?

If you answered "yes" to any of these questions, consult a doctor before doing strenuous exercise.

Also, take special care to progress your running carefully and listen to your body if you are more than 40 years old, or if you have not exercised regularly over the last five years.

swimming

The first of triathlon's three disciplines is, perhaps, it's most technical. The swim section of a triathlon can be anything from 200 meters to several miles (for Ironman races and beyond). Shorter races sometimes take place in local swimming pools, while at longer races you're more likely to swim in open water—a lake, canal, river, or ocean—following a course that's clearly marked with buoys and policed by race marshals in boats or on surfboards, whose central responsibility is to help you stay safe.

Stroke of genius

You can use any stroke you like in a triathlon, but freestyle (front crawl) is the most common. If you're not comfortable swimming freestyle, don't let that stop you getting started, but consider swimming lessons to help you master the stroke (a nose clip and good goggles will also help a great deal—see pages 22–25).

Where to train

The training schedules at the back of this book include specific swim sessions designed to improve both your fitness and technique, so "what" to do isn't going to be a problem. As for where, local swimming pools are the obvious place, and many will have a range of swimming classes or a club that you can join. If you want to train alone, ask if the pool offers lane swimming.

If you're targeting a longer triathlon (standard distance or longer), you'll probably want to practice your open-water and wetsuit swimming. The safest way to do that is to find a supervised venue, perhaps through the list at *www.usaopenwaterswimming.com*. You don't need as much practice in open water as you might think (once a week is probably all you will need to do), and you certainly don't need to swim in open water year round, but it's good to gain confidence, and it's often more interesting than laps in the pool.

HELP! I CAN'T SWIM

The Level 1 and 2 training schedules in this book assume that you can swim at least 200 meters without stopping. If you're not yet able to, find a swim class or coach to teach you, and concentrate on following the rest of the plan. If you need help finding a class, *www.clubswim.com* has a great swimming database that you can search by zip code.

STARTERS ORDERS
Different triathlons have different styles of swim starts. Here's a look at how they work.

TIME TRIAL
Used for: Races in swimming pools.
How it works: Swimmers are sent off at regular intervals, one behind the other. You'll often be asked to estimate your swim time for the race so that race officials can send you off in between other swimmers of similar speeds, so that you don't end up crashing into each other as you swim. Be honest, and use your average training times as a guide.

MASS START
Used for: Open-water races, particularly long-distance ones.
How it works: Everyone gets into the water and lines up behind a series of markers, or they line up on the beach. A horn or gun goes off, and everyone starts together. It can be a bit of a free-for-all until people settle into their swimming, so it's worth picking a position on the edge of the crowd to start from.

WAVE START
Used for: Very large open-water races, or ones where the swim site isn't that large.
How it works: Basically the same as a mass start, but with people broken up into groups and sent off at prearranged times. The groups will often be gender- and age-group-based, giving you a great chance for a bit of realistic age-based competitiveness.

cycling

If you've seen footage of the triathlon at the Olympic Games, you might be expecting a triathlon bike stage to be something like a cycling road race in miniature, and for the professionals it is. But for most of us, triathlon cycling is about riding alone.

Draft dodgers

In the vast majority of triathlon races, it is against the rules to follow someone too closely on the bike (a tactic known as drafting). The rules set down by U.S.A. Triathlon mean that it is against the rules to ride with any part of your bike within the imaginary two-by-seven-meter box surrounding another rider. In practice, that means that you have to stay at least five meters behind the rider in front unless you're obviously overtaking him or her.

IN THE SADDLE

You can race triathlon on any roadworthy bicycle, from a $3,000 Road Trek all the way to a simple model with a basket on the front, but you ideally need to get as much speed as possible from each pedal stroke, and this means that a properly fitted road bicycle, bought from a specialist bike shop, with a few carefully chosen pieces of kit will be best (see pages 26–29).

Where to train

Without doubt, the best place to do your cycling training sessions is on the road. You can use the stationary bikes in a gym, but these won't mirror your position on your race bike very well, and won't give you the road skill and confidence that you'll need on race day.

HELP! I CAN'T CYCLE

If you haven't ridden a bike for a few years, or are completely new to cycling, fear not. Local community centers, schools, and even some bike shops offer cycling proficiency courses to help get things rolling.

TIPS FOR TRIATHLON CYCLISTS

1 Use a map to find routes in your local area, or ask at your local cycling shop or club about quiet roads to train on and organized rides.

2 Always scout out a new route either at an easy pace or in the car; you don't want to go charging around a corner to find yourself faced with an unexpected steep slope.

3 If you're short of practice time, consider commuting to work and back by bicycle. It's a great—and green—way to fit your training around your everyday life.

4 If you're lucky enough to have a training bike and a race bike, have them both set up so that your position is identical on both. You'll race, and feel, much better.

5 Don't avoid learning good road skills just because they're tricky. Cornering and descending at speed, riding with no hands, balancing on the pedals, and even riding out of the saddle are all important skills.

6 Obey the rules of the road at all times. It's not safe or sensible to run red lights, ride on the sidewalk, or cycle without lights at night.

running

The great thing about running is that it's so easy to do. All you really need is a pair of proper running shoes. Here are a few tips to get you going.

Do...
Run often: Frequent short runs are far more effective that infrequent longer ones.

Run outside: Choose routes that allow you to run on smooth dirt trails, cut grass, and tarmac as much as possible.

Run inside: Treadmills are a useful alternative on days when the weather is simply too cold for running outside. They're also useful for teaching you to run with a short, quick stride.

Run hills: Hills are a strong runner's friend. Don't make every run as hilly as possible, but do seek out hills so that you can use them in training.

Run races: Running races are a really easy way to boost your fitness, monitor your progress, and keep you motivated during the winter.

Don't...
Run tired: Apart from a few very specific training sessions, all your runs should be on fresh legs.

Run on concrete: It's too hard a surface to run on for very long without really jarring your body, which can lead to injury.

Run alone at night: If you're going to go running after dark, run with a friend or a club, or at least tell someone where you're going and how long you'll be gone. Always carry your mobile phone, keys, and some money.

Run inside only: There's a whole world of running out there. Get out and see it.

NEVER RUN A STEP?
DON'T WORRY. SIMPLY FOLLOW THIS SIMPLE FOUR-WEEK PLAN.

WEEK ONE

Monday: 15 x 1 min run/1 min walk
Wednesday: 10 x 90 sec run/90 sec walk
Friday: 10 x 2 min run/1 min walk
Sunday: 6 x 3 min run/2 min walk

WEEK TWO

Tuesday: 5 x 4 min run/2 min walk
Thursday: 6 x 4 min run/1 min walk
Saturday: 5 x 5 min run/1 min walk

WEEK THREE

Monday: 4 x 6 min run/1 min walk
Wednesday: 4 x 7 min run/1 min walk
Friday: 3 x 8 min run/1 min walk
Sunday: 3 x 9 min run/1 min walk

WEEK FOUR

Tuesday: 11 min run, 1 min walk, 10 min run,
1 min walk, 9 min run
Thursday: 15 min run, 1 min walk, 14 min run
Saturday: 30 min nonstop run!

equipment

Training and competing in three disciplines requires three sets of equipment, and with variations for training and then racing, the costs can become overwhelming. You need to have running shoes, cycling shoes, running and cycling clothing, a bicycle, swim suit and wet suits, goggles, and that is just the start! So getting sensible advice on what you actually need is critical. In this chapter, you will discover what the absolute necessities are, and which pieces of kit would help you in your training and competing. You will learn how to tailor your equipment list to the event you are taking part in.

swim and race clothing

Simple, durable, and quick-drying kit is essential for both swim training and racing. The items here may be simple, but you'll want to spend some time making sure your choices fit properly and feel good.

TRI SUIT

It may not be the most style-conscious of outfits, but a one-piece, Lycra tri suit works best for most races for both men and women. Look for one with a lightly padded seat area (for comfort on the bike without the "diaper" effect of full cycling shorts), mid-thigh-length legs to prevent chafing, and perhaps a small mesh pocket on the back.

SWIMSUIT

A simple Lycra swimsuit works best for swim training, as it won't bind around you or shift uncomfortably as you swim. The chemicals in most pools don't treat fabrics particularly well, so don't overspend on this—keep it simple, comfortable, and cheap. And, guys, baggies aren't really ideal; if you can't stomach the classic "Speedo," consider a pair of bike-shortlike "jammers."

WETSUIT

An equipment requirement at many races in cooler climates, nonelite triathletes can use a wetsuit in water temperatures up to 84°F (29°C). A proper triathlon wetsuit has a smooth rubberized exterior and will actually help you swim faster as well as keep you warm, so a proper—tight—fit is vital. You can buy a variety of types (even sleeveless), but a full-body suit provides the best protection and the most buoyancy, which will actually help you swim faster.

SWIM ESSENTIALS

The following items aren't swim kit as such, but you'll want to have them with you whenever you head to the pool.

1 Towel (the size is up to you).

2 Plastic bag (to put wet kit in).

3 Shampoo (always wash your skin and hair after swimming, as pool chemicals can irritate the skin).

4 Water bottle (you may be swimming in water, but you'll still need to drink during training).

5 Locker money (or padlock and key).

6 Postswim food (swimming pools always seem to have vending machines, so avoid the temptation by packing a small snack, perhaps an apple or banana).

DO I REALLY NEED A TRI SUIT?

You'll often see newcomers to triathlon struggling to drag T-shirts over damp skin in the transition area after the swim, cursing and sweating as they fight the fabric. It's faster and simpler to buy yourself a tri suit that you can wear comfortably from start to finish.

GOGGLES

Mirrored or tinted goggles will work fine in an indoor pool, and will keep the early morning glare from blinding you in open-water swims. Fit is very individual, so try lots of different pairs, and don't assume that bigger padding always means greater comfort or a better fit. It's how well they seal to your face that counts for preventing leaks.

SWIM HAT

Swim hats do more than keep your hair out of your eyes; they also keep your head (and ears) a little warmer, and at some races different color swim hats are used to identify different start waves. Wear your hat over your goggles when racing. This will stop anyone accidentally pulling your goggles off during the swim.

swim kit

Once you've got the hang of the technique, swimming is a fairly simple activity (stroke, stroke, stroke, breathe. Stroke, stroke ...), but that hasn't stopped the development of an array of training equipment, from wristwatch stroke counters to underwater parachutes. You're certainly not going to need everything, but some equipment will help you get the most out of your time in the pool.

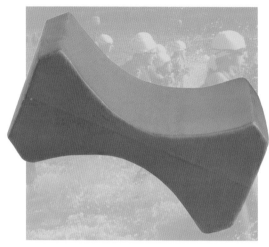

PULL BUOY

This odd-shaped float is designed to fit comfortably and snugly between your thighs to lift your legs in the water and to stop you from kicking. This may seem like cheating, but it actually mimics the effect of a wetsuit reasonably well, as well as forces your arms to do most of the work, so that you learn to catch and hold more water—one of the secrets to good triathlon swimming. Always use it with a band (see below).

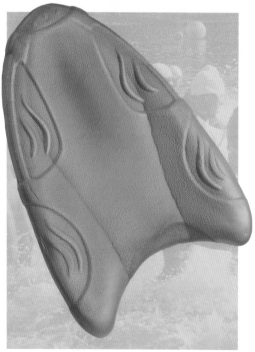

KICK BOARD

Just as a pull buoy shifts the focus to your arms, so a kick board lets you work your legs and develop a smooth, compact, efficient kick. Look for a board that is about the length of your forearms, and hook your hands over the leading edge of it when doing kick drills, so that it pushes your arms and shoulders to the surface.

BAND AID

If you're training with a pull buoy, you should also place a band around your ankles to stop yourself from kicking. To make yourself a band, simply cut 1 foot (30 cm) from an old bicycle inner tube and tie the two cut ends together tightly to create a giant rubber band that will hold your ankles together when you put it on.

EARPLUGS

Swimmer's ear is an annoying condition caused by inflammation in the ear canal owing to trapped water. If it's something you're prone to, simple silicon earplugs can be used to keep water out.

PADDLES

Paddles will vastly increase the amount of water you can "catch" during a stroke, making each stroke more effective, but also greatly increasing the load on your shoulders, arms, and wrists. They're a great tool, but look for small ones that are just larger than your hand and come with a hand and wrist strap. Above all, introduce them into your training gradually (as our schedules do), so that you don't injure yourself.

FINS

Training fins should have a short, stubby fin section and a snug fit around the foot. Used carefully, like paddles, fins can help improve your ankle flexibility and make some of the more technical swimming drills less exhausting to perform.

NOSE CLIP

If you have problems putting your face underwater, or you're prone to sinus problems, a nose clip can be a real help. It should fit tightly and close your nostrils so that water can't get up them. Just remember to breathe through your mouth if you use one!

cycle clothing

You'll probably be spending more time cycling than doing any other discipline. So, in training and in racing, having comfortable, versatile kit is very important.

BIB SHORTS
Padded Lycra cycling shorts will make your training rides much more comfortable, and a pair of "bib shorts" with built-in braces is easily the most comfortable—not least because you won't need to keep pulling them up at the back!

JERSEY
You'll probably need two cycling jerseys in the long run: a short-sleeved one for the summer and a long-sleeved one for the winter. Look for long or full-length zips, and large pockets on the back, so that you have somewhere to store keys, spare inner tubes, ride food, and so on.

WATERPROOF JACKET
A simple, lightweight waterproof jacket with a full-length zip should pack down so small you can stuff it in a back pocket, and it's a whole lot better than a soaking. Get a high-visibility one if you can.

BASE LAYER
Another cold-weather essential, your base layer should take sweat away from your skin, keep you warm even when wet, and not smell too horrific. The best ones are made from Merino wool. Buy a short-sleeved one and team it with arm warmers to create a long-sleeved version for really cold rides.

HELMET

Wearing a protective cycling helmet that meets international safety standards is a requirement at most triathlons and an absolute must-have for safe training. Go for a peakless road-style helmet with plenty of vents to keep your head cool, and wear it level across your brow with the chinstrap securely fastened and not left loose.

DO I NEED SUNGLASSES?

Squinting into the sun as you cycle isn't just uncomfortable, it's dangerous. Find a comfortable pair of shades that don't bounce around or slide down. Get a pair with photochromatic lenses, and you'll be able to wear them to keep the wind, rain, and road spray out of your eyes on dismal days as well.

WARMERS

Ever so useful on days when the weather is changing or it simply starts cold, these simple, brushed-Lycra tubes can be found to cover your arms, knees, even your entire leg.

GLOVES

Classic fingerless cycling gloves aren't a necessity, really, though they're certainly comfortable. But padded, windproof, thermal winter gloves are an absolute must-have for when the weather gets colder.

OVERSHOES

Another winter riding essential, overshoes will keep your feet far warmer than shoes and socks alone. Try to find a pair that is thermal, windproof, and reasonably waterproof.

SHOES

If you're racing using clipless pedals (and we really think you should), you'll need proper cycling shoes. Your shoe should have a stiff sole, and fit snugly around your heel and mid-foot, but there should be about a thumb's width between the end of the shoe and your longest toe, and the shoes certainly should not pinch your feet. Ideally, choose a triathlon-specific model with one large strap and a loop on the heel that you can pull to get the shoe on or off quickly.

cycle kit—bikes and bits

Road bike, mountain bike, hybrid, shopper, cruiser, BMX and tourer—there are bicycles out there for almost every style of cycling you can think of. There are even specially designed triathlon bikes, and if you don't own a bike already, you should seriously consider buying one of these. If they seem a little pricey, consider an entry-level road bicycle instead.

SADDLE

This needs to be comfortable (which doesn't necessarily mean very padded), so choose carefully. If you suffer from numbness "down there" while cycling, consider a saddle with a cutaway central section to relieve the excess pressure.

FRAME

Triathlon bikes tend to have steeper seat tubes than road bikes so that they can be ridden in a more aerodynamic position. The shape of the tube and its material are less important than whether or not it fits you.

WHEELS

You can get some awfully funky aerodynamic carbo wheels. They'll certainly make you go faster, but they're also very expensive, so you're better off with some run-of-the-mill spoked road wheels.

TOP TIP

Keep your tires pumped up and your bike clean and dry, with the chain and gears oiled and free of rust. Ideally, have it professionally serviced at least twice a year.

HANDLEBAR

Road bikes have characteristic curling handlebars, while triathlon bikes tend to have level "bullhorn" bars. Either is acceptable, though the triathlon ones tend to be a little lighter.

AEROBARS

Tucking yourself into a compact, aerodynamic position is one of the easiest ways to go faster. To ride on aerobars, you rest your forearms just above your elbows on the pads, and wrap your hands around the extensions. Ideally, the set you buy should be as adjustable as possible in terms of length, height, width, angle, and pad position so that you can get it just right.

TRAINING TOOLS

You'll be using your bike for both training and racing. So you'll also need:
A bottle cage (or, even better, two) on your bike, and a couple of simple plastic bottles
Lightweight LED front and rear lights
Clip-on mudguards
Puncture repair kit (tire levers, a spare inner tube, and a mini-pump, rather than one of those fiddly kits with glue and patches)

GEAR LEVERS

The gear shifters on a road bike are built into the brake levers. On a triathlon bike they tend to be built into the aerobars so that you can change gears easily while riding.

BRAKES

Your bike should have a front brake and a rear brake, both set up to allow you to stop suddenly or shed speed gradually according to how hard you squeeze the levers. Use your front brake more than your rear one, and keep the pads and wheel rims clean to prevent wear.

COMPUTER

A simple bicycle computer will tell you how fast you're riding, how far you've traveled, and even how fast your feet go around. Use it alongside your heart-rate monitor (see page 32) to measure your effort in training and racing.

PEDALS

You can ride on simple flat pedals or old-fashioned toe clips and straps, but "clipless pedals," matching cleats, and proper cycling shoes to attach them will let you push the pedal around, rather than just stamping down on it. As a result, you'll get more power into the bike and go faster.

run clothing

The only running kit that a triathlete really can't do without is the right running shoes (and a sports bra for ladies). But you'll find running much more comfortable if you invest in some specialized "technical" running kit.

SHORTS

Running shorts come in two styles: loose and light with a built-in brief or tight-fitting Lycra. Either style works well, but try to find a pair with either a small pocket in the waistband or a zipped one in the back so that you can carry keys, energy gels, or other little essentials.

T-SHIRT

Running vests and T-shirts should be made of a lightweight material that takes sweat away from your skin to the surface of the T-shirt, where it can evaporate. This will stop you becoming uncomfortable and reduces the risk of chafing.

TIGHTS

Lycra running tights may take a little getting used to (especially for men), but they're far more comfortable than cold knees.

GILET

You can always use your cycling waterproof jacket for running sessions, but the long sleeves can get a little sweaty. Far more comfortable in all but the most awful conditions is a lightweight running gilet—a sleeveless vest that will keep your torso warm and dry without sacrificing ventilation.

BASE LAYER

There's no need to buy special base layers for running in winter; the ones you buy for cycling should be more than adequate.

SHOE SHOPPING

Buy your running shoes from a specialist running store. Ideally visit them in the afternoon (your feet swell during the day). Try on all the styles suggested and run in them for a few minutes before choosing the most comfortable pair.

WHICH SHOE WILL I NEED?

For a rough idea of which sort of running shoe you should choose, do this simple test.
Dip your bare foot into some water, then step onto a dry floor or piece of paper (don't press your foot down hard, though). The result should look close to one of the following:

NORMAL FOOT

The heel and forefoot prints are attached by a clear band at the mid-foot but the arch area doesn't touch the ground. Most people's feet look like this. You'll probably need shoes with some stability features, but not loads.

FLAT FOOT

You'd think this foot was very stable, but in reality it's collapsing in on itself (overpronating). If your feet are like this, shoe choice is even more important, as you may be very prone to injuries. You'll probably need very supportive shoes with plenty of motion-control features.

HIGH-ARCH FOOT

Are the marks left by your heel and forefoot completely separate or just barely attached? You have a very high arch and a foot that probably doesn't absorb shock very well. You'll probably need flexible shoes with plenty of cushioning, because you may be prone to shin splints.

Triathlon specific running shoes with elastic laces and a toggle are quick and easy to pull on, saving vital seconds in transition 2.

running kit

If you want to get the best out of your runs, and enjoy them as much as possible, you'll want a little more than just basic running essentials like shoes and shorts. A heart-rate monitor will help you train more effectively in all three sports, while hats, gloves, and a way to carry food and drink will keep you comfortable on long runs and in unpleasant conditions.

HEART-RATE MONITOR

Monitoring your pulse as you train will help you gauge how hard you're working in training. In fact, all of our training schedules are laid out using "effort zones" that relate to your heart rate (see pages 50–51 for more details). The best heart-rate monitors include the functions of a sports watch with a lap counter, and can be worn safely when swimming.

FUEL BELT

Waist packs, or these lightweight belts with flasks, allow you to carry vital fuel on long runs and races. The belt should fit snugly and not bounce too much. Ideally, it should have a small pocket for keys, spare change, or blister plasters. Some will even have a holster for a bottle.

SPORTS BRA

A must have for ladies, a proper sports bra will reduce uncomfortable and potentially damaging breast movement by around 60 percent (almost twice the movement reduction of a normal bra). Look for one designed for high-impact activities, and wear it for cycling, racing, and running.

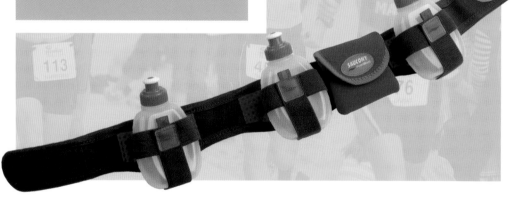

CROSS DRESSING!

Some bits of kit can easily be used for more than one sport. Running tights can be worn over bike shorts on cold days. Cycling base layers can be worn on the run. In a pinch, you can even swim in your running shorts. Buying for three sports tends to mean more kit, so make your purchases carefully, avoiding really expensive versions of things that will quickly wear out (like cycle shorts and socks).

HEADWEAR

If you're running outside you'll need two hats. The first is a simple thermal beanie to keep your head and ears warm in winter. The second is a lightweight peaked cap to protect your head from sunstroke and your eyes from bright sunshine in the summer.

SOCKS

Also made of "technical" wicking materials, running socks come in many different styles. If you're prone to blisters, consider a thin double-layer pair, and invest in some wool/nylon mix running socks for winter, as these will keep your feet warm when wet.

WATER BOTTLE

When you are running for more than 30 minutes, you should increase your fluid levels as you run. A simple hand-held bottle is ideal—though be careful that the larger ones don't unbalance your running style.

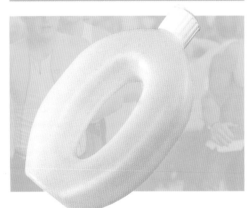

GLOVES

A winter-training essential, lightweight thermal gloves will protect your hands from windchill and stop you losing heat too quickly when it's cold or wet. Find a pair that can easily be bunched up and stuffed in a pocket mid-run if things warm up.

racing stripes

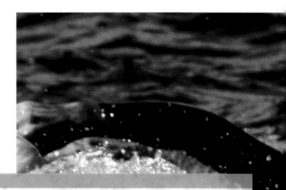

On race day you're going to need bits of kit for all three disciplines, plus a few special pieces that will make your life easier. The checklist on this page should cover all the bases, so you may want to copy it out and tick things off as you load the car.

RACE KIT CHECKLIST

FOR EVERYTHING:

Tri suit
Heart-rate monitor or sports watch
Number belt
Sports bra (ladies!)
Bodyglide (to prevent chafing in any sensitive areas!)

FOR YOUR WARM-UP:

Comfortable running clothing
A bottle of sports drink to sip
An energy gel for before the swim

FOR THE SWIM:

Goggles
Swim hat
Nose clip (if you use one)
Wetsuit (for open-water swims)
A towel (to stand on in transition)

FOR THE BIKE:

Bicycle
Helmet
Cycling shoes
Socks
Sunglasses
Bottles of sports drinks

FOR THE RUN:

Running shoes
Socks (take two pairs!)
Energy gels in a fuel belt or waist pack

OTHER BITS:

Track pump
Chain lube (and cloth to clean the chain first)
Strong sunscreen
Postrace treat

For tricks and tips that should make race day run smoothly, turn to page 126.

OTHER USEFUL KIT

TRACK PUMP

It's far easier to pump tires with one of these than a little hand pump. It should even have a pressure gauge so you know when to stop pumping. (Run your tires at about 8 bar or 120 psi, making sure you pump them up the morning of the race.)

CHAIN LUBE

Spray cans of chain lube are the easiest way to keep your gears running smoothly. Clean your chain and gears the night before your race, and wipe them down and oil them before you leave your bike in transition, taking care not to get oil on your tires or braking surfaces.

NUMBER BELT

You'll need a number on your back on the bike and on your front on the run. You can pin them to your tri suit, but they can get in the way during the swim, so you're better off with a number belt. Attach your race number to the belt, and leave it lying on top of your helmet in transition. Just don't forget to put it on!

DRUGS IN SPORT!

If you're asthmatic, or on any form of medication that you might need mid-race, always, always, always carry it with you, and tell the race marshals as well.

food for thought

Whether you are training to improve your performance or to take part in a race, one of the the most vital ingredients is diet. Good sports nutrition will help you prepare and compete to the best of your ability. It will also keep your muscles topped up with glycogen, and your body well hydrated. This chapter will show you how to create a balanced daily diet that will complement your training, and how to to eat and drink effectively around a training session.

macronutrients

Food and triathlon go hand in hand. You'll be training solidly, several times a week, sometimes even several times a day, for an event that lasts at least an hour, and every workout you do is going to burn fuel. As a result, what you eat, how much you eat, and when you eat it is going to be crucial. In this chapter, you'll find healthy eating strategies, guidance on how much to eat and drink, and tips on eating in and around training and racing. Just remember, food should be healthy and fun, so don't chain yourself to an extreme diet that you won't be able to sustain.

MACRONUTRIENTS

CARBOHYDRATES

Carbohydrates are the main source of fuel for triathletes, and come in two types. Simple carbs, like sugars, are quickly drawn into the body and broken down for fuel. Complex carbs are called starches, and take time to break down, providing a lower level of energy over a much longer period. Aim to get 40–60 percent of your calories from carbohydrates, most of which should be taken in just before, sometimes during, and particularly after your training sessions. Focus on getting the majority from fresh fruit and vegetables, with smaller amounts from potatoes, basmati rice, pulses, and wholewheat pasta and bread. There are roughly four calories per gram of carbohydrate.

PROTEIN

Absolutely vital if you want to recover well after training, protect your body from illness, and build stronger, fitter muscles, bones, and tendons, protein should provide 20–30 percent of your daily calories. Make lean meats, chicken, and fish, as well as nuts, pulses, and low-fat dairy a part of every meal you eat. There are roughly four calories per gram of protein.

FAT

Fat fuels our life when we're not training, helps us absorb vitamins A, D, E, and K, and protects our organs. Use the mono- and polyunsaturated oils in nuts, olive oil, avocados, and oily fish like salmon, mackerel, and trout to provide 20–30 percent of your daily calories. Avoid all hydrogenated, partially hydrogenated, and low-grade saturated fats as much as possible. There are roughly nine calories per gram of fat.

WATER

Lose just one percent of your body's water and you'll reduce your physical and mental performance by closer to 10 percent, so aim to stay hydrated throughout the day (see pages 40–41 for more on hydration and exercise).

MICRONUTRIENTS

Vitamins, minerals, and other trace nutrients keep us healthy in ways that we're only beginning to understand. B vitamins help us process food into fuel, omega-3 fats fight inflammation, and the phytonutrients in broccoli, spinach, and even red wine help combat diseases like cancer.

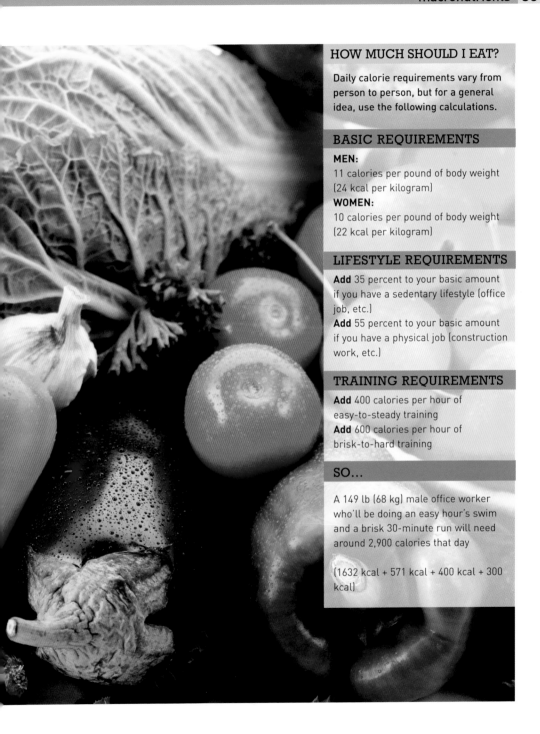

HOW MUCH SHOULD I EAT?

Daily calorie requirements vary from person to person, but for a general idea, use the following calculations.

BASIC REQUIREMENTS

MEN:
11 calories per pound of body weight (24 kcal per kilogram)
WOMEN:
10 calories per pound of body weight (22 kcal per kilogram)

LIFESTYLE REQUIREMENTS

Add 35 percent to your basic amount if you have a sedentary lifestyle (office job, etc.)
Add 55 percent to your basic amount if you have a physical job (construction work, etc.)

TRAINING REQUIREMENTS

Add 400 calories per hour of easy-to-steady training
Add 600 calories per hour of brisk-to-hard training

SO...

A 149 lb (68 kg) male office worker who'll be doing an easy hour's swim and a brisk 30-minute run will need around 2,900 calories that day

(1632 kcal + 571 kcal + 400 kcal + 300 kcal)

water relief

Without wishing to sound relentlessly depressing, dehydration will kill you far quicker than starvation. Even at low levels, it impairs performance by an alarming amount. So it'll come as no surprise that staying adequately hydrated throughout the day is good for fitness and for health.

DRINKING HABITS

1 Set a pattern for what, when, and how much you drink, and you'll find your training performances and recovery both improve.

2 Start and end every day with a glass of water, and drink another glass with each meal.

3 Take a drink with you for any training session lasting 60 minutes or more, and take small sips every 10–20 minutes.

4 Use an electrolyte-based sports drink mixed to a 5–7 percent solution, rather than water, as your training drink.

5 For shorter sessions, simply have a glass of water before you start.

6 To get an exact amount of how much you dehydrate during training, weigh yourself before and after. For every pound less you weigh you need to drink a pint of water.

7 Monitor the color of your urine. When you're properly hydrated, it will be a very pale yellow.

8 Always clean your teeth when you get home after a training session where you've been drinking sports drinks.

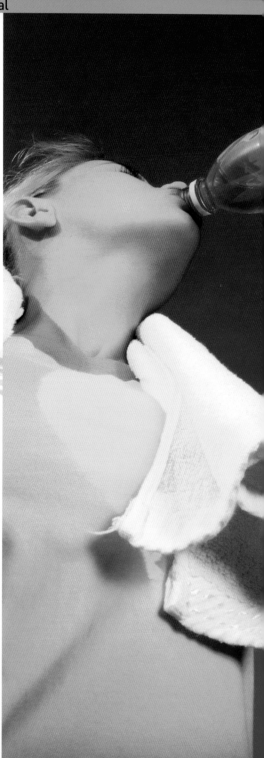

SPORTS DRINKS

Gatorade, SiS, High 5, Powerbar, Infinit—several companies make special sports drinks. Some come ready made, but you're better off with the powdered versions that you mix yourself. Good sports drinks will contain carbohydrates for fuel (ideally, a mix of sugars and maltodextrin) as well as sodium, potassium, and other electrolytes to replace those lost through sweat. They needn't contain protein, vitamins, amino acids, or caffeine. Try as many flavors as possible to find one you like best.

HYDRATION Q & A

DO COFFEE AND TEA COUNT?

Yes. The caffeine in tea and even strong coffee isn't enough to dehydrate you more than the fluid in the cup will hydrate you. Steer clear of creamy, sugary drinks, though, as these just add "empty" calories to your diet.

WHAT ABOUT BOOZE?

You don't have to be teetotal to train, but high alcohol intakes are neither healthy nor sensible, so moderation is advised. That said, the trace chemicals in red wine and dark beers have actually been shown to improve health, so the odd "medicinal" glass is fine.

WHAT ABOUT SODA?

Diet or not, carbonated drinks are packed with processed chemicals and acidic compounds that aren't much good for your gut or for your health. If you don't like plain water, drink diluted fruit juice or iced water with sliced lemon for flavor.

CAN I DRINK TOO MUCH?

There have been a few "overhydration" scare stories in the media—particularly in relation to marathon running—and, yes, it's certainly possible. Let thirst and sweat rate guide your fluid intake, remembering that only the largest of us will need, or be able to take in, two pints an hour, and then only in very hot conditions.

the meal deal

Fitting healthy eating into a hectic lifestyle can be tough enough without factoring in training sessions. To make it all a little simpler, here are some sample daily diets for different training situations:

HEALTHY EATING TIPS

1 Don't stuff yourself at every meal, but eat well immediately after training.

2 Eat smaller meals and more snacks rather than a few large meals.

3 Aim for five portions of fruit AND five portions of vegetables every day (frozen, canned, and dried all count).

4 Have a post-training snack within 15 minutes of finishing a hard training session or race. This should be low in fat and contain roughly 1 gram of protein for every 4 grams of carbohydrate. Several sports nutrition companies make powdered "recovery" drinks that are ideal.

5 Don't add salt to your food.

6 Avoid microwave-ready meals and processed foods as much as possible.

7 Snack on nuts and fruit rather than cookies and cakes.

8 Ideally, take a multivitamin and mineral, as well as a high-strength omega-3 supplement, every day.

9 If you struggle with "bad" foods, consider treating yourself once a week with anything you feel like, perhaps after your hardest or least favorite training session.

REST DAY

Breakfast: Fruit salad with unsweetened yogurt and toasted almonds OR
Two-egg, ham, and mushroom omelette with grilled tomatoes and a glass of orange juice

Lunch: Large tuna salad with roasted red pepper, green beans, sliced scallions and tomatoes, a few olives, and an olive oil and balsamic vinegar dressing OR
A pint of chicken and vegetable soup and a yogurt with dried fruit

Dinner: Beef stir-fry with mixed vegetables and cashew nuts, plus a small serving of rice OR
Roast chicken with carrots, broccoli, roast squash, and potatoes

Snacks (throughout the day): Six to eight walnuts, four pieces of fruit, and some low-salt beef jerky

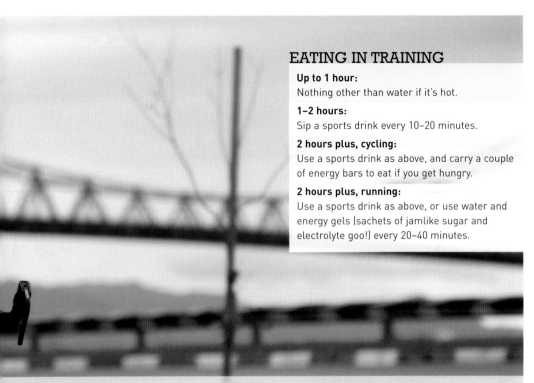

EATING IN TRAINING

Up to 1 hour:
Nothing other than water if it's hot.

1–2 hours:
Sip a sports drink every 10–20 minutes.

2 hours plus, cycling:
Use a sports drink as above, and carry a couple of energy bars to eat if you get hungry.

2 hours plus, running:
Use a sports drink as above, or use water and energy gels (sachets of jamlike sugar and electrolyte goo!) every 20–40 minutes.

MORNING TRAINING

Presession snack: A glass of fruit juice and a yogurt with dried fruit

Postsession breakfast: Oatmeal with skim milk, honey, and a banana OR
Wholewheat English muffins with cashew or almond butter

Lunch: Beef chili with green salad and a baked potato OR
Chicken and avocado wrap with spinach, tomatoes, and roasted onions

Dinner: Large piece of grilled salmon with asparagus, broccoli, and peas OR
Lean lamb skewers with roasted Mediterranean vegetables

Snacks (throughout the day): 10–12 almonds, an orange, and a large handful of dried fruit

TWO-SESSION DAY

Presession snack: A large glass of fruit juice and a banana

Postsession breakfast: Two to four slices of wholewheat toast with a poached egg and a glass of milk OR A large, low-fat bean burrito

Lunch: A Mediterranean vegetable and ham pasta salad with two pieces of fruit OR Two multiseed bagels with low-fat cream cheese, pastrami, tomato, pickles, and a large glass of orange juice

Presession snack: A fruit smoothie

Postsession dinner: Pasta with bolognese sauce and salad OR Thin-crust vegetable pizza with low-fat cheese

Snacks (throughout the day): Two sliced apples with cashew butter, a mixed berry smoothie, and some fresh pineapple

recipe for success

TWO DAYS BEFORE

Dinnertime two days out from your race is when you start to prime your fuel cells for the big day. Have a generous carbohydrate-rich meal, such as pasta and sauce or rice, this evening and have an extra glass of water with your meal.

THE DAY BEFORE

Both breakfast and lunch today should be high-carbohydrate meals similar to yesterday's supper, but dinner should be a smaller, normal meal so that you don't wake tomorrow feeling bloated and unwell. Use fruit juice or a weak sports drink to stay hydrated today, rather than just water.

RACE-DAY BREAKFAST

Assuming that you're racing in the morning, you'll aim to finish breakfast at least three hours before the event starts—even if it means getting up very early! Nerves may make your stomach quite sensitive today, but eat your tried-and-tested prerace high-carb breakfast (oatmeal with honey and bananas, or white toast with peanut butter and jelly are typical choices, but you should use what suits your stomach). Don't forget to drink some water or a weak sports drink with your meal.

PREPARING FOR THE RACE

You shouldn't need to eat anything between breakfast and the start of your race, but sip a weak sports drink to stay hydrated. Don't drink too much, just enough to keep thirst at bay.

BEFORE YOU START

Once you're warmed up and ready to line up for the start, you may want to take an energy gel to lift your blood sugar for the swim. Don't drink or eat very much, though, because that could lead to stomach cramps.

What and how you eat on the day of a race should be slightly different from what and how you eat on a normal training day. You're going to want to head to the start line fully fueled but not so stuffed that you feel sluggish. And in the race itself, you're going to need to stay hydrated and keep your blood sugar topped up so that you don't run out of energy before the finish line. Here's what to do:

IN THE SWIM

It's not really possible to eat here, but try to avoid swallowing too much water!

OUT ON THE BIKE

It's tempting to drink or eat something as soon as you finish the swim, but it's not a good idea. Your blood will start reflowing when you stand up out of the water, and it can take a while for things to settle. Only start drinking or taking gels after you've been on the bike for a while (5–10 minutes for short races, 15–20 minutes for middle and long distances), then drink regularly according to your plan. Unless you're racing a very long event, you should aim to carry all the fuel you'll need for the bike leg of your race with you on your bike. Make sure you finish it!

ONTO THE RUN

It's harder to take in fuel or fluids when running, so energy gels are really useful here. Make sure you have a little water with them to wash them down, either from a bottle of your own or from the aid stations on the course.

POSTRACE

You may find it quite difficult to stomach food after a race, but you should eat and drink something once you've got your breath back. The best things to eat are the typically healthy foods you'll find on pages 42 and 43, but if you feel like treating yourself, go ahead.

HOW MUCH FUEL WILL I NEED?

The human body can absorb about 1 gram of carbohydrate per minute irrespective of body size, so aim to take that much fuel on for every hour you're racing. You could get that from:

two pints of sports drink at 6 percent solution,
two or three energy gels,
one-and-a-half energy bars,
or any combination of those.

TRIED AND TESTED!

Never eat anything the day before or on the morning of a race that you haven't tested in and around training. A great way to do this is to try out a few different prerace meals on the evening before your longest training session, and to experiment with different makes, flavors, concentrations, and volumes of sports drink and energy gels during training in the weeks building up to your race. Try taking small amounts every 10 minutes and larger amounts every 20 minutes. Try energy bars and water, and try sports drinks alone. Keep experimenting until you find a fueling strategy that suits you. Then stick with it.

train smart

Whether you are an experienced triathlete with several Ironman competitions under your belt, or a complete novice, you need to train correctly. Learning how to combine swim, run, and cycle training in your program can make all the difference to your performance. In this chapter, you will learn how to develop your speed, strength, and stamina, how to monitor your fitness levels for each discipline, and how to practice transitions. Finally, you will learn how to avoid injury, stay motivated, and enjoy training and competing for years to come.

catch the train

Successful races are built up from days and weeks of successful training sessions. And training successfully isn't simply a matter of getting out the door. Here are some simple training rules to keep in mind as you follow your chosen schedule.

TRI-TRAINING'S GOLDEN RULES

1   STICK TO THE PLAN

The training schedules in this book offer a balance of work and rest, easy workouts and hard training, and a careful buildup of workouts given in a particular order. Each workout has a purpose, so, ideally, do them exactly as they are listed.

2   BE CONSISTENT

If you have to miss the occasional workout, don't worry too much, but try not to miss large chunks of your plan. Jumping in and out of a training program when you feel like it won't build your fitness effectively, and could even leave you at risk of injury.

3   BE HONEST

Assuming you're not ill or injured, if the day's training calls for a hard session, do the hard session. If you don't think you can manage it, head out and give it a try—starting with a nice long warm-up.

4   WARM UP AND COOL DOWN

All of the workouts in the training sessions include a minimum of five minutes at an easy effort at the start as a warm-up and another five minutes easy at the end. If a specific, longer warm-up is given, take it, but if nothing is listed still do the two five-minute blocks.

5   TREAT YOUR INJURIES

If you're unfortunate enough to get injured or become ill during your training, don't worry. Stop training, get treatment as soon as possible, and follow the advice of your doctor or physical therapist. Return to your program where you left off when it is appropriate.

SAMPLE TRAINING SESSIONS

You'll find a whole range of different training sessions in our schedules, but, broadly speaking, they fall into the following six categories.

RECOVERY ▶▶ Easy workouts aren't a waste of time. They burn calories, they encourage tired muscles to loosen, and they let you concentrate fully on the technical aspects of each sport. Above all, they give you time to enjoy exercise without worrying about speed.

ENDURANCE ▶▶ These sessions build your ability to work without stopping for the length of your race, train your body to store and burn fuel more effectively, strengthen your heart, and—for running—"tune" your muscles so that they can handle the impact of many strides.

RACE EFFORT ▶▶ Workouts at your intended race pace will leave you comfortable settling into the right pace come race day. Ideally, do these sessions over terrain and in conditions similar to those you'll face on race day, right down to what and how much you eat and drink.

BRISK EFFORT ▶▶ Building your best possible aerobic engine is the major factor in getting fit for racing. There's no more effective way to do this than working just below your functional threshold—a "comfortably hard" pace, just a little easier than the best pace you could hold for an hour.

INTERVALS ▶▶ Blocks of work with set rests after each are a classic method of improving your speed and raising your fitness to a new level. Intervals strengthen your cardiovascular system and teach your body to handle anaerobic efforts without needing to slow down too much.

BURSTS ▶▶ Short, sharp efforts of no more than a minute strengthen your muscles, tendons, and even bones, and train your body to convert energy into movement quickly, effectively, and without wastage.

in the zone

Okay, you've started looking for a race, you've got your shiny new kit, and you've filled your cupboards with healthy, tasty food. You're probably itching to pick a plan and get started training. But before you head out the door, you'll need to figure out how hard to workout.

Take it to the limit

Effective training isn't about pushing yourself to your absolute limit day after day; it's about consistent work, gradual increases, and knowing how hard you can safely push. The schedules on pages 64–103 are all set out by time or distance (mainly for the swim), and how hard you should work is indicated by an effort level between Easy and Very Hard. Each level emphasizes different aspects of your fitness, and is used for different types of session.

With these levels, all you have to do is focus on staying in the right one for the length of time indicated. You could use feeling to guide you, but it's far more effective to tie each effort to a range of pulse rates using a heart-rate monitor (see page 32).

TO WORK OUT A ROUGH THRESHOLD HEART RATE, USE THE FORMULA
0.85 x (214-(0.8 x age) for men
0.85 x (209-(0.9 x age) for women

Then simply calculate the percentage "ranges" for each level using the figures in the table below.

SWIM LEVELS

Setting levels for swimming works a little differently, because it's hard to use a heart-rate monitor in a pool. Our lower-level training schedules are built around race-pace swimming, so all you have to do is "guesstimate" how fast you'll be able to swim come race day, and there's a simple race-pace test session at the start of each program to guide you. In the more advanced schedules, you should be setting your paces based on your swim times from recent sprint-distance races, because your average pace per 100 meters in a sprint race should be pretty close to your threshold pace. Five seconds faster per 100 meters is Hard, five seconds slower per 100 meters is Steady. Easy is as slow as you like, and Very Hard as fast as you can.

IT FEELS...	USE IT FOR...	% THRESHOLD HEART RATE
EASY	warm-ups, cool-downs, and long workouts	69–83%
STEADY	more challenging long workouts and short-endurance sessions	84–94%
BRISK	threshold training and very long intervals	95%–105%
HARD	traditional "speedwork" intervals	106%+
VERY HARD	bursts and other short, sharp efforts	N/A

SETTING LEVELS FROM RACING

Wearing a heart-rate monitor in races will help you pace your effort evenly, and it'll also give you a more accurate idea of your threshold. If you push yourself in a sprint or supersprint race, you'll probably average an effort very close to your true threshold. So, you should use that number to calculate your training zones rather than the formula above.

staying out of trouble

Training for a triathlon means that, at times, you're going to have to push yourself outside of your comfort zone. But that doesn't mean that you should train through a sprained ankle or a chest infection. It can take a long time to fully understand all the many signals that your body will send you before, during, and after training, so here are some simple rules to keep you out of trouble.

STAY SAFE

The world isn't always as safe as we might like. Always carry identification and your mobile phone when you're cycling or running, and always let someone know where you're going and how long you'll be.

GET PHYSICAL

If an injury doesn't ease after a day or so of no training, or flares up again during a workout, book a session with a physical therapist as soon as possible. Ideally, find one who specializes in treating sports injuries and put your trust in him or her.

BUILD UP SLOWLY

Trying to pile on more training than you can safely handle, or suddenly increasing the amount you're doing, will leave you open to illness, injury, and excessive fatigue. If you're following the schedules and have to miss more than one or two sessions, pick up where you left off, don't skip ahead to where you think you should be. If you're building your own training, never increase what you do by more than 10 percent per session per week.

DON'T RUN TIRED

Short of crashing your bike, running tired is the easiest way to get injured. Don't stack two hard run days back to back, or do a long run the day after a long or hard bike ride. And, if you're going to run and ride in the same day, always run first unless the schedule specifically tells you not to.

TAKE YOUR RESTS

The schedules contain rest days, easier weeks, and even breaks within training sessions. Stick to them, even if you think you don't need them, because it's better to rest a little before you have to than not to rest enough.

TWEAKS AND TWINGES

If you feel a tweak that you think might be a real injury in the making, follow these four simple steps.

Rest: Stop the session immediately, get home, take your weight off the affected area, and try to keep it as still and comfortable as possible.

Ice: Wrap an ice pack (or even a bag of frozen peas) in a damp towel, and hold it firmly against the injured area for 10–15 minutes every hour to reduce any swelling associated with the injury. You can also try taking a nonsteroidal anti-inflammatory, such as ibuprofen.

Compression: Wrapping the injury in a compression bandage will help support it and help reduce any swelling. Just don't tie the bandage too tight!

Elevation: Raising your injury above your heart restricts the blood flow to it, which can prevent excessive swelling and damage.

STRETCH GENTLY

Vigorous stretching before and after exercise might seem like a good idea, but it's not. By all means stretch gently after exercise, and perhaps in the evening before you go to bed, but don't force yourself deeper than is comfortable and never, ever stretch before exercise. See pages 56–57 for some good stretches.

WASH YOUR HANDS

Regular training can make you more prone to catch any bugs going around, so make a real effort to keep your hands clean so that you don't transfer germs from things you touch. Use antibacterial hand wash in the kitchen and bathroom, and keep a tub of alcohol hand cleanser in a desk drawer or your bag.

EAT AND DRINK HEALTHILY

Proper nutrition can boost your immune system and even help prevent some injuries. Follow the healthy eating guidelines on pages 38–45, and make especially sure that you eat a recovery meal within 15 minutes of finishing any hard training sessions or races.

going strong

There's no doubt that doing a couple of short, quite intense weight-training sessions per week is a good idea from an overall health viewpoint. But it won't have a major impact on your triathlon performance. More important for triathlon is core stability and muscular control, which you'll develop with exercises like these.

STEP-DOWN

Stand sideways on a step, feet hip-width apart with one foot on the step and the other foot "floating" in mid-air, level with the step. Keeping your body still and upright, and your arms by your sides, slowly lower your "floating" foot back down to the floor by bending your other knee and ankle. Touch the sole of your foot to the floor, then straighten the leg, and return to the start position. 3 x 10 reps for each leg.

PIKES

Start in a traditional push-up position with your arms straight. Keeping your spine, shoulders, legs, and head in line, lift your right hand off the floor and rotate your hips and shoulders out to the right. Pause when your raised arm and shoulders are perpendicular to the floor, then slowly rotate back around, put the hand down, and repeat on the other side. To increase the challenge, do a simple push-up between each side of the pike. 3 x 10 reps.

POWER PLAY

To get the best out of a gym workout, lift fairly heavy weights for only a few repetitions, and focus on "compound" moves using free weights. Ask your gym instructor to teach you the proper form for the following, and do three sets of 6–8 repetitions for each.

Deadlifts
Step-back lunges
Step-ups
Upright rows
Shoulder presses
Power cleans

SIDE PLANKS

Lie on your side, then push yourself up so that you are resting on the side of your foot and one elbow and forearm, and so that your chest and hips are at right angles to the floor. Pull your stomach muscles in and lift your hip off the floor into line with your legs and torso. Hold this for 10 seconds, then slowly lower yourself until your hip just touches the floor. Pause, then lift yourself up for another 10 seconds. 10 reps for each side.

ONE-LEG BRIDGE

Lie on your back with your knees bent, the soles of your feet flat on the ground, and your arms by your sides. Push your hips off the floor until they form a straight slope with your thighs, chest, and shoulders. Now lift one foot off the floor and straighten that leg, keeping the thighs in line and together. Hold for 15–30 seconds, then bring the foot back to the floor and switch legs so that the other one is straightened. Hold again, then lower your hips back to the floor to rest. 3 x 30–60 seconds.

going long

Each training session you do should be followed by some gentle stretching. You won't recover faster because of it, but it should ease some of the discomfort you may feel and allow you to maintain a normal range of motion.

CALVES

Step forward into a lunge position and push your trailing heel back into the floor with the leg straight. Hold for 30–45 seconds, then shift your weight back and bend the back leg slightly to stretch your soleus. Hold this for 30–45 seconds, then switch legs.

CHEST

Stand upright and lift your arms up in front of you until they are level with your shoulders. Take a deep breath in as you spread your arms wide and push your chest forward. Breathe out slowly, trying to open the chest still further.

BACK AND SHOULDERS

Stand up straight and bring your elbows together in front of your chest. Place your right elbow in the crook of your left elbow, twist your arms around each other, and clasp your hands together. Gently pull your forearms and hands away from your chest and face. Hold, then unravel and switch the left arm to the top.

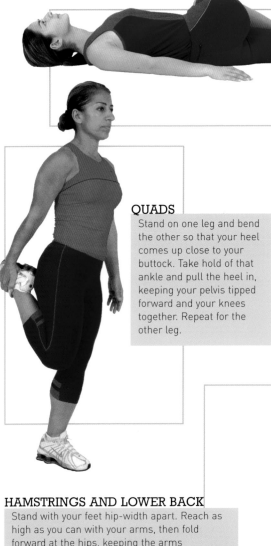

GLUTES

Lie on your back with your legs straight and bend one knee. Grasp your bent leg with both hands halfway down the shin, and pull the knee in toward the center of your chest. Hold the stretch for 20–30 seconds. After holding that stretch, grab the still-bent knee with the opposite hand and pull it down across your body so that your hips rotate and the knee is pushed across the body and toward the floor.

QUADS

Stand on one leg and bend the other so that your heel comes up close to your buttock. Take hold of that ankle and pull the heel in, keeping your pelvis tipped forward and your knees together. Repeat for the other leg.

HAMSTRINGS AND LOWER BACK

Stand with your feet hip-width apart. Reach as high as you can with your arms, then fold forward at the hips, keeping the arms outstretched, until you are bent forward, looking at your knees with your arms hanging down in front of you. Hang here for 30–45 seconds, then straighten up by "rolling" up your spine from bottom to top.

eager to tri

One of the great things about triathlon training is that it comes with a built-in motivation tool—your target race. You want to reach race day fit and prepared to produce the performance all your hard work deserves. But, even so, there will be days when summoning the will to train will be quite hard. A few missed days here and there aren't a problem, but you don't want to get into a routine of avoiding your training sessions.

Follow a plan

Training schedules give shape and purpose to your training, give you lots of little goals to achieve, and provide a variety of sessions to build your fitness and keep you interested. They also take the worry out of workouts, because all you have to do is follow the instructions.

Keep a log

In the back of this book, you'll find a training diary. Use it to keep records of each session you do, how it felt, what your heart rates and speeds were, and even what the weather was like. Look back over it from time to time to remind yourself how far you've come.

Break it down

Your target race can seem a long way off, so set yourself some little targets to hit along the way. These can be training-focused (e.g., average 18 mph on a long bike ride) or even other events—a middle-distance race if you're building up to Ironman, or a 10 km running race. You'll find incidental races like these included in many of our schedules.

Train with others

Training in a group is a great motivator. You'll have a reason to keep to the plan, a little healthy competition, and someone to talk to on long rides and runs. Organize some like-minded friends or colleagues into a triathlon team and train for the same event, or see if you can find a triathlon club near you.

Whatever you do, remember to have fun. Triathlon is a challenge, certainly, but it should be a fun challenge. If you feel yourself starting to lose sight of that, stop, relax, leave your watch at home, and just head out and train as hard as you want for as long as you want.

FUN FIXES

Need to boost your enthusiasm for training? Here are some other things you might try:

1 Schedule a coffee-shop stop. Train hard, and then treat yourself to a favorite snack before you head home.

2 Write out all of your training sessions, or photocopy them, and put a big red tick through each one after you've done it.

3 Low motivation can be a sign of fatigue. Take an extra day off, do something fun with family or friends, eat well, and get a good night's sleep.

4 Help out at a local race. The energizing mix of effort and enjoyment of those taking part is surprisingly infectious.

5 Watch some great performances on T.V. Watching riders battling up a mountain in the Tour de France or olympians swim gives you an example to follow.

6 Treat yourself to some new training kit—there's nothing like having a new toy to play with.

7 Stuck in a rut in a long session? Switch from plodding at the same pace to a "soft fartlek" session. Fartlek means "speed-play," so lift the pace for as long as you like, then drop back, recover, and do another effort. Each effort or recovery can be as long as you like, just don't push too hard.

the schedules

The secret to enjoying your training and making solid progress is to follow a well devised schedule. This means giving yourself a working framework, with goals that are realistic and achievable. Just going out on the bike, or for a run, or to the pool, and training until you get tired, is a recipe for losing interest and giving up. Keeping to your plan and reaching the goals you set yourself will ensure that you stay motivated.

This chapter provides day-by-day training programs at six levels of ability, to help you achieve your training and racing goals effectively and without injury. We also look at the simple principles of training that all triathletes should adhere to, whether or not they are working to a training schedule.

how the schedules work

There are six different training schedules laid out across the next 40 pages. Each focuses on a different goal, and each contains a slightly different balance and volume of training. The levels can be worked through over time, from level one to level six as you get gradually fitter or your goals change,

or you can "drop in" and start with the level that's appropriate to you.

which schedule to choose

You'll need to be able to cope with a certain amount of training from the very start of each schedule. The

1 STARTER LEVEL	**2** STARTER LEVEL	**3** INTERMEDIATE LEVEL
PAGES 64–67	PAGES 68–71	PAGES 72–77
for complete beginners	**for beginners who have been training for a while or have completed a shorter race**	**for newcomers looking to improve their performance over short distances**
TARGET: Your choice of a novice event, supersprint, or sprint race.	**TARGET:** Your first short-course (Olympic) triathlon	**TARGET:** A new sprint race personal record
YOU NEED TO BE ABLE TO:	**YOU NEED TO BE ABLE TO:**	**YOU NEED TO BE ABLE TO:**
■ Train for up to six hours a week	■ Train for up to eight hours a week	■ Train for up to 10 hours a week
■ Fit in up to six training sessions a week	■ Fit in up to six training sessions a week	■ Fit in up to nine training sessions a week
■ Swim at least 400 meters without stopping	■ Swim at least 400 meters without stopping	■ Swim at least 1,000 meters without stopping
■ Run for 30 minutes without stopping	■ Run for 45 minutes without stopping	■ Run for 60 minutes without stopping
■ Cycle for 60 minutes without stopping	■ Cycle for 60 minutes without stopping	■ Cycle for two hours without stopping

exact amounts are set out below, and if you can't yet meet the requirements for the plan you'd like to follow, your best course of action will be to take an honest step back, look at the levels again, meet that goal, and then move up to the next.

SKILLS AND DRILLS

Some of the sessions in the schedules include specific drills or types of session, from swim drills to bricks. You'll find out what these are and how do them on pages 104–107.

---

4 INTERMEDIATE LEVEL

PAGES 78–83

for experienced triathletes who have completed at least one short-course (Olympic) race

TARGET:
A faster short-course performance

YOU NEED TO BE ABLE TO:

■ Train for up to 12 hours a week

■ Fit in up to 10 training sessions a week

■ Swim at least 1,500 meters without stopping

■ Run for 90 minutes without stopping

■ Cycle for three hours without stopping

---

5 EXPERT LEVEL

PAGES 84–91

for experienced triathletes who have completed several short-course (Olympic) races

TARGET:
Your first middle-distance triathlon

YOU NEED TO BE ABLE TO:

■ Train for up to 10 hours a week

■ Fit in up to 12 training sessions a week

■ Swim at least 1,500 meters without stopping

■ Run for 90 minutes without stopping

■ Cycle for three hours without stopping

---

6 EXPERT LEVEL

PAGES 92–103

for experienced triathletes who have completed middle-distance races and want the ultimate challenge

TARGET:
Your first Ironman-distance triathlon

YOU NEED TO BE ABLE TO:

■ Train for up to 18 hours a week

■ Fit in up to 12 training sessions a week

■ Swim at least 2,000 meters without stopping

■ Run for 90 minutes without stopping

■ Cycle for four hours without stopping

starter level

Never done a triathlon before? This is where you start. This eight-week plan will gradually build you up to the point where you can complete your first race.

It may sound like an impossible task at this stage, but with a little focus and determination you'll find your fitness levels rise surprisingly quickly.

what if ... I'm really fit?

Everyone has different strengths and weaknesses. If you're one of those lucky people who has no problem running a six-minute mile or cycling at 20 miles an hour, great. Make the most of your speed without stepping outside the requirements of the scheduled sessions. It's easy to underestimate how hard you're working.

WHICH RACE SHOULD I CHOOSE?

It's up to you whether you choose to start your triathlon campaign with a novice race, supersprint, or sprint, but you'll probably want to choose based on the length of swim or run you feel capable of. (Turn back to pages 12–13 for a look at what the different race distances involve.)

RACE EFFORT

A number of workouts in the schedule ask you to work at Race Effort. You'll have nothing to compare to for your first race, so you'll have to pick a speed that you think you can sustain for the race distance. The effort should feel "comfortably hard," or brisk rather than hard (see pages 48–49).

	MONDAY	TUESDAY
WEEK 1	swim 2 x 50 m easy, 4 x 25 m hard, 2 x 200 m race effort, 2 x 50 m easy. Take 20 secs rest after each short effort, one minute after each 200 m	run 20 mins steady
WEEK 2	swim 10 x 75 m with 15 secs rest after each (do the first and last two easy and the rest at race effort)	run 22 mins steady
WEEK 3	swim 6 x 150 m with 15 secs rest after each (do the first and last easy and the rest at race effort)	run 25 mins steady

WEEK 4 RECOVERY WEEK	MONDAY	TUESDAY	
	rest	swim 2 x 50 m easy, 4 x 25 m hard, 2 x 200 m race effort, 2 x 50 m easy. Take 20 secs rest after each short effort and one minute after each 200 m	

CATCH-UP

To swim "catch-up" simply take a stroke with your right arm while leaving the left outstretched in front of you like Superman. Touch your thumbs together when the right arm reaches the front, then leave the arm outstretched while you take a stroke with your left arm. Make sure you bend your elbow as your stroking arm comes out of the water to recover.

SPEED CHECK

When cycling, remember to work by effort and heart rate, not speed. Your speed will be affected by hills, gusts of wind, and even road surfaces, so you shouldn't expect it to stay the same throughout the ride.

WEDNESDAY	THURSDAY	FRIDAY	SATURDAY	SUNDAY
bike 40 mins steady (use your gears to keep a cadence of 85–95 rpm throughout)	swim 16 x 50 m catch-up (see below) with 15 secs rest after each (do the first and last four easy and the rest at race effort)	run 20 mins steady	rest	bike 40 mins steady (find a quiet, rolling route, keep your effort and cadence constant up and down hills)
bike 45 mins (5 mins easy, then steady at 85–95 rpm with 10-sec very hard seated bursts in the same gear every 5 mins, then 5 mins easy)	swim 8 x 100 m catch-up with 15 secs rest after each (do the first and last two easy and the rest at race effort)	run 22 mins steady	rest	bike 50 mins (5 mins easy, then steady at 85–95 rpm with 10-sec very hard seated bursts in the same gear every 5 mins, then 5 mins easy)
bike 55 mins (5 mins easy, then steady at 85–95 rpm but with a 12-sec very hard seated burst in the same gear every 5 mins, then 5 mins easy)	swim 4 x 200 m catch-up with 15 secs rest after each (do the first and last easy and the rest at race effort)	run 25 mins steady	rest	bike 60 mins (10 mins easy, then pick up to the sort of effort you hope to ride at in your race and hold it for 40 mins, then 10 mins easy)

WEDNESDAY	THURSDAY	FRIDAY	SATURDAY	SUNDAY
run 20 mins steady	swim 16 x 50 m catch-up with 15 secs rest after each (do the first and last four easy and the rest at race effort)	run 20 mins steady	rest	bike 40 mins steady

starter level continued

You should be feeling the benefits of the first four weeks of training. Now it's time to step up a gear, and work toward your first competitive race.

	MONDAY	TUESDAY
WEEK 5	swim 4 x 200 m with 15 secs rest after each (do the first and last easy and the rest at race effort)	run 27 mins steady
WEEK 6	swim 3 x 300 m with 15 secs rest after each (start the first one nice and easy, and aim to make each 300 m faster than the one before)	run 30 mins steady
WEEK 7	swim 800 m nonstop (start easy, build to race pace by halfway, then hold it until the last 100 m, which you can swim easy)	run 33 mins steady

WEEK 8	MONDAY	TUESDAY
RACE WEEK	rest	swim 14 x 50 m with 15 secs rest after each (do the first and last four easy and the rest at race effort)

CATCH-UP REMINDER

To swim "catch-up" simply take a stroke with your right arm while leaving the left outstretched in front of you like Superman. Touch your thumbs together when the right arm reaches the front, then leave the arm outstretched while you take a stroke with your left arm. Make sure you bend your elbow as your stroking arm comes out of the water to recover.

WEDNESDAY	THURSDAY	FRIDAY	SATURDAY	SUNDAY
bike 60 mins steady (5 mins easy, then steady at 85–95 rpm but with a 15-sec very hard seated burst in the same gear every 5 mins, then 5 mins easy)	swim 3 x 250 m with 15 secs rest after each (start the first one nice and easy as catch-up, then just swim, aim to make each 250 m faster than the one before)	run 27 mins steady	rest	bike 70 mins steady (5 mins easy, then steady at 85–95 rpm but with a 15-sec very hard seated burst in the same gear every 5 mins, then 5 mins easy)
bike 60 mins steady (5 mins easy, then steady at 85–95 rpm but with a 20-sec very hard seated burst in the same gear every 5 mins, then 5 mins easy)	swim 2 x 400 m with 15 secs rest after each (start the first one easy, alternating 50 m swim with 50 m catch-up, the second one at race effort)	run 30 mins steady	rest	bike 80 mins steady (5 mins easy, then steady at 85–95 rpm but with a 20-sec very hard seated burst in the same gear every 5 mins, then 5 mins easy)
bike 60 mins steady (5 mins easy, then steady at 85–95 rpm but with a 20-sec very hard seated burst in the same gear every 5 mins, then 5 mins easy)	swim 4 x (50 m swim, 50 m catch-up, 50 m swim, 50 m hard with 15 secs rest after each)	run 33 mins steady	rest	bike 90 mins steady (5 mins easy, then steady at 85–95 rpm but with a 20-sec very hard seated burst in the same gear every 5 mins, then 5 mins easy)

WEDNESDAY	THURSDAY	FRIDAY	SATURDAY	SUNDAY
run 20 mins steady	rest	bike 40 mins easy (include 4 x 1 min at race effort with 4 mins easy after each)	rest	**RACE** (stick to your paces and race your own race until the last half of the run, then give it whatever you've got!)

starter level

Standard-distance triathlons, at 2-3 hours in duration, may be twice the length of a sprint race, but they are still within the reach of the first-timer.

This schedule covers 12 weeks, and will gradually build up your swimming, cycling, and running endurance to the level you'll need to cover 1,500 m of swimming, 25 miles of cycling, and a 10-km run.

WHAT IF ...

This isn't my first race?
If you've successfully completed a standard-distance race before, and are aiming to get faster over the distance, you'll probably want to look at the training schedule in level four (see pages 78–83). If all you've done are novice, supersprint, and sprint races, you're probably better off sticking with the schedule below.

WEEK	MONDAY	TUESDAY	WEDNESDAY
1	run 30 mins easy	swim 2 x 50 m easy, 4 x 25 m hard, 2 x 400 m race effort, 2 x 50 m easy. Take 20 secs rest after each short effort and one minute after each 400 m	bike 60 mins easy
2	run 40 mins easy	swim 4 x 100 m easy with 15 secs rest after each, then 20 x 50 m pull (see p104) at race effort with 20 secs rest after each. Finish with 4 x 50 m easy, every fourth 50 m catch-up	bike 60 mins steady (5 mins easy, then steady 85–95 rpm with a 10-sec hard burst every 5 mins)
3	run 50 mins easy	swim 4 x 100 m easy with 15 secs rest after each, then 20 x 50 m pull at race effort with 15 secs rest after each. Finish with 4 x 50 m easy. Swim every fourth 50 catch-up	bike 60 mins steady (5 mins easy, then steady 85–95 rpm with a 15-sec hard burst every 5 mins)
4 *(RECOVERY)*	run 30 mins easy	swim 4 x 100 m easy with 15 secs rest after each, then 15 x 50 m pull at race effort with 20 secs rest after each. Finish with 4 x 50 m easy	bike 60 mins easy or rest
5	run 50 mins easy	swim 4 x 100 m easy with 15 secs rest after each, then 20 x 50 m pull at race effort with 15 secs rest after each. Finish with 4 x 50 m easy; swim every fourth 50 m catch-up	bike 60 mins steady (5 mins easy, then steady 85–95 rpm with a 15-sec hard burst every 5 mins)
6	run 60 mins easy	swim 4 x 100 m easy with 15 secs rest after each, then 20 x 50 m pull at race effort with 10 secs rest after each. Finish with 4 x 50 m easy; swim every fourth 50 m catch-up	bike 60 mins steady (5 mins easy, then steady 85–95 rpm with a 20-sec hard burst every 5 mins)

DON'T OVERWORK

Every fourth week in this schedule is a recovery week, and contains only a few short workouts. This is to give your body a little extra time to rebuild itself, so don't add extra workouts in just because you feel you're not doing enough.

TIME TRIAL

Use the average pace you hold for the 1,000 m time-trial swim in Week 4 as your new Race Effort for swimming.

THURSDAY	FRIDAY	SATURDAY	SUNDAY
swim 200 m easy with every fourth 25 m backstroke, then 15 x (50 m race effort, 50 m catch-up (see below) with 10 secs rest after each). Finish with 4 x 25 m easy	run 30 mins as 10 mins easy, 10 mins brisk, 10 mins easy	bike 60 mins easy to steady	rest
swim 200 m easy with every fourth 25 m backstroke, then 15 x 100 m race effort with 10 secs rest after each. Finish with 4 x 25 m easy	run 30 mins as 10 mins easy, 10 mins brisk, 10 mins easy	bike 90 mins easy to steady	rest
swim 200 m easy with every fourth 25 m backstroke, then 10 x 150 m race effort with 10 secs rest after each. Finish with 4 x 25 m easy	run 30 mins as 10 mins easy, 10 mins brisk, 10 mins easy	bike 2 hrs easy to steady	rest
swim 2 x 50 m easy, 4 x 25 m hard, 1,000 m time trial, 2 x 50 m easy	run 30 mins easy to steady	bike 60 mins easy to steady	rest
swim 200 m easy with every fourth 25 m backstroke, then 15 x 100 m race effort with 10 secs rest after each. Finish with 4 x 25 m easy	run 40 mins as 12 mins easy, 3 x 5 mins brisk with 1 min easy jog after each, 10 mins easy	bike 90 mins easy to steady	rest
swim 200 m easy with every fourth 25 m backstroke, then 10 x 150 m race effort with 10 secs rest after each. Finish with 4 x 25 m easy	run 40 mins as 12 mins easy, 3 x 5 mins brisk with 1 min easy jog after each, 10 mins easy	bike 2 hrs easy to steady	rest

starter level continued

PACE YOURSELF

Keep a close eye on your times during the swim sets. If your target Race Effort is 1:45/100 m, you want to swim all the reps at that pace. Don't hammer the first couple just because you're fresh.

TIME TRIAL

Use the average pace you hold for the 1,500 m time-trial swim in Week 8 as your new Race Effort for swimming.

WEEK		MONDAY	TUESDAY	WEDNESDAY	
7		run 70 mins easy	swim 4 x 100 m easy with 15 secs rest after each, then 20 x 50 m pull at race effort with 10 secs rest after each. Finish with 4 x 50 m easy; swim every fourth 50 catch-up	bike 60 mins steady (5 mins easy, then steady 85–95 rpm with a 25-sec very hard seated burst in the same gear every 5 mins, then 5 mins easy)	
8	RECOVERY	run 30 mins easy	swim 4 x 100 m easy with 15 secs rest after each, then 15 x 50 m pull at race effort with 20 secs rest after each. Finish with 4 x 50 m easy	bike 60 mins easy or rest	
9		run 70 mins easy	swim 4 x 100 m easy with 15 secs rest after each, then 20 x 50 m pull at race effort with 15 secs rest after each. Finish with 4 x 50 m easy; swim every fourth 50 m catch-up	bike 60 mins steady (5 mins easy, then steady at 85–95 rpm but with a 15-sec very hard seated burst in the same gear every 5 mins, then 5 mins easy)	
10		run 80 mins easy	swim 4 x 100 m easy with 15 secs rest after each, then 20 x 50 m pull at race effort with 10 secs rest after each. Finish with 4 x 50 m easy; swim every fourth 50 m catch-up	bike 60 mins steady (5 mins easy, then steady at 85–95 rpm but with a 25-sec very hard seated burst in the same gear every 5 mins, then 5 mins easy)	
11		run 90 mins easy	swim 4 x 100 m easy with 15 secs rest after each, then 20 x 50 m pull at race effort with 5 secs rest after each. Finish with 4 x 50 m easy; swim every fourth 50 m catch-up	bike 60 mins steady (5 mins easy, then steady at 85–95 rpm but with a 25-sec very hard seated burst in the same gear every 5 mins, then 5 mins easy)	
12	RACE WEEK	run 45-60 mins easy (don't push yourself!)	rest	bike 60 mins easy (include 3 x 1 min at race effort with 4 mins easy after each, and 3 x 30 secs hard with 4.5 mins after each)	

THURSDAY	FRIDAY	SATURDAY	SUNDAY
swim 200 m easy with every fourth 25 m backstroke, then 8 x 200 m race effort with 10 secs rest after each. Finish with 4 x 25 m easy	run 40 mins as 12 mins easy, 3 x 5 mins brisk with 1 min easy jog after each, 10 mins easy	bike 2 hrs 30 mins easy to steady	rest
swim 2 x 50 m easy, 4 x 25 m hard, 1,500 m time trial, 2 x 50 m easy	run 30 mins easy to steady	bike 90 mins easy to steady	rest
swim 200 m easy with every fourth 25 m backstroke, then 10 x 150 m race effort with 10 secs rest after each. Finish with 4 x 25 m easy	run 45 mins as 12 mins easy, 4 x 5 mins brisk with 1 min easy jog after each, 10 mins easy	bike 2 hrs easy to steady	rest
swim 200 m easy with every fourth 25 m backstroke, then 8 x 200 m race effort with 10 secs rest after each. Finish with 4 x 25 m easy	run 40 mins as 12 mins easy, 4 x 5 mins brisk with 1 min easy jog after each, 10 mins easy	bike 2 hrs 30 mins easy to steady	rest
swim 200 m easy with every fourth 25 m backstroke, then 6 x 250 m race effort with 10 secs rest after each. Finish with 4 x 25 m easy	run 40 mins as 12 mins easy, 4 x 5 mins brisk with 1 min easy jog after each, 10 mins easy	bike 3 hrs easy to steady	rest
swim 200 m easy with every fourth 25 m backstroke, then 20 x 50 m race effort with 10 secs rest after each. Finish with 4 x 25 m easy	bike 30 mins easy (stay on the flat and keep the cadence at 85–95 rpm)	rest	**RACE DAY!**

mastering the sprint

Once you've got a couple of novice and sprint-distance races under your belt, you'll probably find your ambitions turning from "just finishing" to beating your best times so far. This 12-week program is designed to help you do just that.

WEEK	MONDAY	TUESDAY	WEDNESDAY	THURSDAY
1	rest	**AM** bike 60 mins easy to steady; **PM** run (10 mins easy, then 14 x 1 min hard with 30 secs walk after each, then 10 mins easy)	swim 4 x 100 m easy with 15 secs rest after each, then 3 x (10 x 25 m pull (see page 104) then 1 x 200 m hard swim. Take 20 secs rest after each 25 m, and 3 mins after each 200 m). Finish with 4 x 50 m easy	**AM** run (10 mins easy, 3 x 5 mins brisk, 1 min easy after each, then 10 mins easy); **PM** bike (10 mins easy, then 40 mins steady at 85–95 rpm with a 20-sec very hard seated burst in same gear every 5 mins, then 10 mins easy)
2	rest	**AM** bike (20 mins easy, then 2 x 10 mins brisk, 5 mins easy between, then 15 mins easy); **PM** run (10 mins easy, then 10 x 90 secs hard, 30 secs walk after each, then 10 mins easy)	swim 4 x 100 m easy with 15 secs rest after each, then 3 x (10 x 25 m pull, then 1 x 200 m hard swim. Take 20 secs rest after each 25 m, and 3 mins after each 200 m). Finish with 4 x 50 m easy. Do the first set of 25 m as pull with paddles	**AM** run (10 mins easy, 3 x 5 mins brisk, 1 min easy after each, then 10 mins easy); **PM** bike (10 mins easy, then 40 mins steady at 85–95 rpm, with a 20-sec very hard seated burst in the same gear every 5 mins, then 10 mins easy)
3	rest	**AM** bike (20 mins easy, then 2 x 10 mins brisk with 5 mins easy in between, then 15 mins easy); **PM** run (10 mins easy, then 8 x 2 mins hard with 30 secs walk after each, then 10 mins easy)	swim 4 x 100 m easy with 15 secs rest after each, then 3 x (10 x 25 m pull, then 1 x 200 m hard swim. Take 20 secs rest after each 25 m, and 3 mins after each 200 m). Finish with 4 x 50 m easy. Do the first two sets of 25 m as pull with paddles	**AM** run (10 mins easy, 3 x 5 mins brisk with 1 min easy after each, then 10 mins easy); **PM** bike (10 mins easy, then 40 mins steady at 85–95 rpm, but with a 20-sec very hard seated burst in the same gear every 5 mins, then 10 mins easy)
4	rest	**AM** bike 60 mins easy; **PM** run 20 mins easy	swim 1,000 m easy with every fourth length backstroke	run (10 mins easy, then 10 x 30 secs hard with 1 min easy after each, then 5 mins easy)

Training the sprint

It may be the shortest of the four classic triathlon distances, but the "sprint-distance" race really isn't a sprint. Even the fastest triathletes will take about an hour to finish one, which means that the keys to a fast performance are going to be the ability to swim quickly without going flat out, to cycle fast without destroying your legs for the run, to hit the run hard and fast from the moment you get off the bike, and—across all sports—the ability to work effectively at efforts right at and even above your threshold.

FRIDAY	SATURDAY	SUNDAY
AM run (10 mins easy, 3 x 5 mins brisk, 1 min easy after each, then 10 mins easy); **PM** bike (10 mins easy, then 40 mins steady at 85–95 rpm, with 20-sec very hard seated burst every 5 mins, then 10 mins easy), swim (4 x 100 m easy, 15 secs rest after each, then 8 x 150 m as 50 m hard, 75 m brisk, 25 m very hard. Take 40 secs rest after each 150 m). Finish with 4 x 50 m easy; run (10 mins easy, 3 x 5 mins brisk, 1 min easy after each, then 10 mins easy); bike (10 mins easy, then 40 mins steady at 85–95 rpm, with a 20-sec very hard seated burst in the same gear every 5 mins, then 10 mins easy), run 40 mins easy	**AM** bike (20 mins easy, then 2 x 10 mins brisk with 5 mins easy in between, then 15 mins easy); **PM** swim 400 m easy with every fourth length backstroke, 24 x 50 m steady pull with 10 secs rest after each. Finish with 4 x 50 m easy	bike 2hrs easy to steady, straight into run (5 mins brisk, then 5 mins easy)
AM swim 4 x 100 m easy with 15 secs rest after each, then 8 x 150 m as 50 m hard, 75 m brisk, 25 m very hard. Take 35 secs rest after each 150 m. Finish with 4 x 50 m easy; **PM** run (20 mins easy, 20 mins steady)	**AM** bike (20 mins easy, then 2 x 10 mins brisk with 5 mins easy in between, then 15 mins easy); **PM** swim 400 m easy with every fourth length backstroke, 26 x 50 m steady pull, 10 secs rest after each. Finish with 4 x 50 m easy	bike 2hrs easy to steady, straight into run (10 mins brisk, then 5 mins easy)
AM swim 4 x 100 m easy with 15 secs rest after each, then 8 x 150 m as 50 m hard, 75 m brisk, 25 m very hard. Take 30 secs rest after each 150 m. Finish with 4 x 50 m easy; **PM** run (10 mins easy, 10 mins steady, 10 mins brisk, 10 mins easy)	**AM** bike (20 mins easy, then 2 x 10 mins brisk with 5 mins easy in between, then 15 mins easy); **PM** swim 400 m easy with every fourth length backstroke, 28 x 50 m steady pull with 10 secs rest after each. Finish with 4 x 50 m easy	bike 2hrs easy to steady, straight into run (15 mins brisk, then 5 mins easy)
AM swim 20 x 50 m easy with 15 secs rest after each. Do every fourth 50 m hard; **PM** run 20 mins easy	bike 60 mins easy (include 3 x 1 min at race effort, 4 mins easy after each, and 3 x 30 secs hard, 4.5 mins easy after each)	short running race (5 km to 10 km) or bike time trial (10 to 25 miles)

mastering the sprint continued

Setting the pace

Use your swim time from a recent sprint or supersprint race to calculate your swim training paces. Your race pace is your brisk pace, 5 seconds faster per 100 m is hard, 5 seconds slower is steady, and easy is anything slower than that.

WEEK	MONDAY	TUESDAY	WEDNESDAY	THURSDAY
5	rest	**AM** bike (20 mins easy, then 20 mins brisk, then 20 mins easy); **PM** run (10 mins easy, then 15 x 1 min hard with 30 secs walk after each, then 10 mins easy)	swim 4 x 100 m easy with 15 secs rest after each, then 3 x (10 x 25 m pull, then 1 x 200m hard swim. Take 20 secs rest after each 25 m, and 3 mins after each 200 m). Finish with 4 x 50 m easy. Do the first set of 25 m as pull with paddles	**AM** run (10 mins easy, 4 x 5 mins brisk with 1 min easy after each, then 10 mins easy); **PM** bike (10 mins easy, then 40 mins steady at 85–95 rpm with 20-sec very hard seated burst in the same gear every 5 mins, then 10 mins easy)
6	rest	**AM** bike (20 mins easy, then 20 mins brisk, then 20 mins easy); **PM** run (10 mins easy, then 11 x 90 secs hard with 30 secs walk after each, then 10 mins easy)	swim 4 x 100m easy with 15 secs rest after each, then 3 x (10 x 25m pull, then 1 x 200m hard swim. Take 20 secs rest after each 25 m, and 3 mins after each 200 m). Finish with 4 x 50 m easy. Do the first two sets of 25 m as pull with paddles	**AM** run (10 mins easy, 4 x 5 mins brisk with 1 min easy after each, then 10 mins easy); **PM** bike (10 mins easy, then 40 mins steady at 85–95 rpm but with a 20 sec very hard seated burst in the same gear every 5 mins, then 10 mins easy)
7	rest	**AM** bike (20 mins easy, then 20 mins brisk, then 20 mins easy); **PM** run (10 mins easy, then 9 x 2 mins hard with 30 secs walk after each, then 10 mins easy)	swim 4 x 100 m easy with 15 secs rest after each, then 3 x (10 x 25 m pull, then 1 x 200m hard swim. Take 20 secs rest after each 25 m, and 3 mins after each 200 m). Finish with 4 x 50 m easy. Do all three sets of 25 m as pull with paddles	**AM** run (10 mins easy, 4 x 5 mins brisk with 1 min easy after each, then 10 mins easy); **PM** bike (10 mins easy, then 40 mins steady at 85–95 rpm with a 20-sec very hard seated burst in the same gear every 5 mins, then 10 mins easy)
8	rest	**AM** bike 60 mins easy; **PM** run 20 mins easy	swim 1,000 m easy with every fourth length backstroke	run (10 mins easy, then 10 x 30 secs hard with 1 min easy after each, then 5 mins easy)

RECOVERY

SPOT YOUR WEAKNESSES

Use the races in Weeks 4 and 8 to work on whichever of the two options you're weakest in, try out different prerace meals, and generally get used to the nervous energy of racing.

FRIDAY	SATURDAY	SUNDAY
AM swim 4 x 100 m easy with 15 secs rest after each, then 6 x 200 m as 50 m hard, 100 m brisk, 50 m very hard. Take 40 secs rest after each 150 m. Finish with 4 x 50 m easy; PM run (10 mins easy, 10 mins steady, 15 mins brisk, 10 mins easy)	AM bike (20 mins easy, then 20 mins brisk, then 20 mins easy); PM swim 400 m easy with every fourth length backstroke, 10 x 100m steady pull with 10 secs rest after each. Finish with 4 x 50 m easy	bike 2hrs easy to steady, straight into run (10 mins brisk, then 5 mins easy)
AM swim 4 x 100m easy with 15 secs rest after each, then 6 x 200m as 50m hard, 100m brisk, 50m very hard. Take 35 secs rest after each 150. Finish with 4 x 50m easy; PM run (10 mins easy, 10 mins steady, 10 mins brisk, 5 mins hard, then 10 mins easy)	AM bike (20 mins easy, then 20 mins brisk, then 20 mins easy); PM swim 400 m easy with every fourth length backstroke, 12 x 100 m steady pull with 10 secs rest after each. Finish with 4 x 50 m easy	bike 2hrs easy to steady, straight into run (15 mins brisk, then 5 mins easy)
AM swim 4 x 100 m easy with 15 secs rest after each, then 6 x 200 m as 50 m hard, 100 m brisk, 50 m very hard. Take 30 secs rest after each 150 m. Finish with 4 x 50 m easy; PM run (10 mins easy, 10 mins steady, 10 mins brisk, 10 mins hard, 5 mins easy)	AM bike (20 mins easy, then 20 mins brisk, then 20 mins easy); PM swim 400 m easy with every fourth length backstroke, 14 x 100 m steady pull with 10 secs rest after each. Finish with 4 x 50 m easy	bike 2hrs easy to steady, straight into run (20 mins brisk, then 5 mins easy)
AM swim 20 x 50 m easy with 15 secs rest after each. Do every fourth 50 m hard; PM run 20 mins easy	bike 60 mins easy (include 3 x 1 min at race effort with 4 mins easy after each, and 3 x 30 secs hard with 4.5 mins after each)	short running race (5 km to 10 km) or bike time trial (10 to 25 miles)

mastering the sprint continued

WEEK	MONDAY	TUESDAY	WEDNESDAY	THURSDAY
9	rest	**AM** bike (20 mins easy, then 25 mins brisk, then 15 mins easy); **PM** run (10 mins easy, then 16 x 1 min hard with 30 secs walk after each, then 10 mins easy)	swim 4 x 100 m easy with 15 secs rest after each, then 3 x (10 x 25 m pull, then 1 x 200 m hard swim. Take 20 secs rest after each 25 m, and 3 mins after each 200 m). Finish with 4 x 50 m easy. Do all three sets of 25 m as pull with paddles	bike (30 mins easy, 15 mins steady, 10 mins brisk, 5 mins easy), straight into run (5 mins brisk, 5 mins hard, 5 mins easy)
10	rest	**AM** bike (20 mins easy, then 25 mins brisk, then 15 mins easy); **PM** run (10 mins easy, then 12 x 90 secs hard with 30 secs walk after each, then 10 mins easy)	swim 4 x 100 m easy with 15 secs rest after each, then 3 x (10 x 25 m pull, then 1 x 200 m hard swim. Take 20 secs rest after each 25 m, and 3 mins after each 200 m). Finish with 4 x 50 m easy. Do all three sets of 25 m as pull with paddles	bike (30 mins easy, 15 mins steady, 10 mins brisk, 5 mins easy), straight into run (10 mins brisk, 5 mins hard, 5 mins easy)
11	rest	**AM** bike (20 mins easy, then 25 mins brisk, then 15 mins easy); **PM** run (10 mins easy, then 10 x 2 mins hard with 30 secs walk after each, then 10 mins easy)	swim 4 x 100 m easy with 15 secs rest after each, then 3 x (10 x 25 m pull, then 1 x 200 m hard swim. Take 20 secs rest after each 25 m, and 3 mins after each 200 m). Finish with 4 x 50 m easy. Do all three sets of 25 m as pull with paddles	bike (30 mins easy, 15 mins steady, 10 mins brisk, 5 mins easy), straight into run (15 mins brisk, 5 mins hard, 5 mins easy)
12	rest	**AM** swim 20 x 50 m easy with 15 secs rest after each. Do every fourth 50 m hard; **PM** run (10 mins easy, then 10 x 30 secs hard with 1 min easy after each, then 5 mins easy)	bike 60 mins easy	**AM** swim 20 x 50 m easy with 15 secs rest after each. Do every fourth 50 m hard; **PM** run 20 mins easy

RACE WEEK

EASY TRANSITION

Unless otherwise instructed, keep your cycling cadence between 85 and 90 rpm most of the time, and try to get used to running with a quick, light stride and a running cadence of 90 or more. This way, when you combine the two in races, you'll find running fast off your bike much easier.

FRIDAY	SATURDAY	SUNDAY
AM swim 4 x 100 m easy with 15 secs rest after each, then 4 x 300 m as 50 m hard, 200 m brisk, 50 m very hard. Take 40 secs rest after each 150 m. Finish with 4 x 50 m easy; **PM** run (10 mins easy, 10 mins steady, 10 mins brisk, 5 mins hard, then 10 mins easy)	**AM** bike (20 mins easy, then 25 mins brisk, then 15 mins easy); **PM** swim 400 m easy with every fourth length backstroke, 8 x 150 m steady pull with 10 secs rest after each. Finish with 4 x 50 m easy	bike 2hrs easy to steady, straight into run (15 mins brisk, then 5 mins easy)
AM swim 4 x 100 m easy with 15 secs rest after each, then 4 x 300 m as 50 m hard, 200 m brisk, 50 m very hard. Take 35 secs rest after each 150 m. Finish with 4 x 50 m easy; **PM** run (10 mins easy, 10 mins steady, 10 mins brisk, 10 mins hard, 5 mins easy)	**AM** bike (20 mins easy, then 25 mins brisk, then 15 mins easy); **PM** swim 400 m easy with every fourth length backstroke, 9 x 150 m steady pull with 10 secs rest after each. Finish with 4 x 50 m easy	bike 2hrs easy to steady, straight into run (20 mins brisk, then 5 mins easy)
AM swim 4 x 100 m easy with 15 secs rest after each, then 4 x 300 m as 50 m hard, 200 m brisk, 50 m very hard. Take 30 secs rest after each 150 m. Finish with 4 x 50 m easy; **PM** run (10 mins easy, 10 mins steady, 10 mins brisk, 10 mins hard, 5 mins easy)	**AM** bike (20 mins easy, then 25 mins brisk, then 15 mins easy); **PM** swim 400 m easy with every fourth length backstroke, 10 x 150 m steady pull with 10 secs rest after each. Finish with 4 x 50 m easy	bike 2hrs easy to steady, straight into run (25 mins brisk, then 5 mins easy)
rest	bike 60 mins easy (include 3 x 1 min at race effort with 4 mins easy after each, and 3 x 30 secs hard with 4.5 mins after each)	**RACE**

tackling the Olympic

Standard-distance triathlons are surprisingly hard to race really well. Each of the individual legs of the race is now long enough to seriously derail your overall performance if you go too hard. Follow the 12-week plan below, though, and you'll not only build the fitness you need, you'll also learn how to pace yourself properly on race day.

WEEK	MONDAY	TUESDAY	WEDNESDAY	
1	**AM** run 60 mins easy; **PM** swim 4 x 100 m easy with 15 secs rest after each, then 3 x (12 x 25 m pull, then 1 x 200 m hard swim. Take 20 secs rest after each 25m, and 3 mins after each 200 m, and do every fifth 25 m hard). Finish with 4 x 50 m easy	bike 60 mins easy (include 3 x 5 mins in a big gear *(see above)*, alternating 5 secs very hard with 25 secs easy at 40–60 rpm. Take 5 mins easy between blocks)	**AM** run (10 mins easy, then 8 x 90 secs hard with 30 secs walk after each, then 10 mins easy); **PM** swim 400 m easy with every fourth length backstroke, 30 x 50 m steady with 10 secs rest after each. Finish with 4 x 50 m easy	

	MONDAY	TUESDAY	WEDNESDAY	
2	rest	**AM** run 70 mins (55 mins easy, 5 mins steady, 5 mins brisk, 5 mins easy); **PM** swim 4 x 100 m easy, 15 secs rest after each, then 3 x (12 x 25 m pull, then 1 x 200 m hard swim. Take 20 secs rest after each 25 m, and 3 mins after each 200 m, and do every fifth 25 hard). Finish with 4 x 50 m easy, first set of 25 m as pull with paddles	bike 60 mins easy (include 2 x 8 mins in a big gear, alternating 5 secs very hard with 25 secs easy at 40–60 rpm. Take 5 mins easy between blocks)	
3	rest	**AM** run 80 mins (65 mins easy, 5 mins steady, 5 mins brisk, 5 mins easy); **PM** swim 4 x 100 m easy with 15 secs rest after each, then 3 x (12 x 25 m pull, then 1 x 200 m hard swim. Take 20 secs rest after each 25 m, and 3 mins after each 200 m, and do every fifth 25 m hard). Finish with 4 x 50 m easy. Do the first two sets of 25 m as pull with paddles	bike 60 mins easy (include 2 x 10 mins in a big gear, alternating 5 secs very hard with 25 secs easy at 40–60 rpm. Take 5 mins easy between blocks)	

	MONDAY	TUESDAY	WEDNESDAY	
4	rest	**AM** run 60 mins easy; **PM** swim 4 x 100 m easy with 15 secs rest after each, then 3 x (8 x 25 m pull, then 1 x 200 m hard swim. Take 20 secs rest after each 25 m, and 3 mins after each 200 m). Finish with 4 x 50 m easy. No paddles!	bike 60 mins easy at 80–90 rpm (include 8 x 20-sec very hard seated bursts with about 5 mins easy after each)	

RECOVERY

BIG GEAR

Your Big Gear cycling session (Tuesday in Week 1, but otherwise Wednesday) should be done on the turbo trainer or along a flat, quiet road. Warm up at 85–95 rpm, then ride in a gear big enough to give you a cadence of just 40–60 rpm when riding easy, and stay seated in your aero position throughout the ride—certainly for each block of efforts.

THURSDAY	FRIDAY	SATURDAY	SUNDAY
rest	AM run 30 mins easy; PM bike (5 mins easy, 50 mins steady, 5 mins easy)	swim 400 m easy with every fourth length backstroke, 30 x 50 m steady pull with 10 secs rest after each. Finish with 4 x 50 m easy	bike 2hrs easy to steady at 80–90 rpm, straight into run (10 mins brisk, then 5 mins easy)

THURSDAY	FRIDAY	SATURDAY	SUNDAY
AM run (10 mins easy, then 10 x 90 secs hard with 30 secs walk after each, then 10 mins easy); PM swim 400 m easy with every 4th length backstroke, 30 x 50m steady with 10 secs rest after each. Finish with a 4 x 50m easy	AM run (15 mins easy, 15 mins steady); PM bike (5 mins easy, 20 mins steady, 10 mins brisk, 20 mins steady, 5 mins easy)	AM run (15 mins easy, 15 mins steady); PM bike (5 mins easy, 20 mins steady, 10 mins brisk, 20 mins steady, 5 mins easy)	bike 2 hrs 15 mins easy to steady at 80–90 rpm, straight into run (15 mins brisk, then 5 mins easy)
AM run (10 mins easy, then 12 x 90 secs hard with 30 secs walk after each, then 10 mins easy); PM swim 400 m easy with every fourth length backstroke, 30 x 50 m steady with 10 secs rest after each. Finish with 4 x 50 m easy	AM run (10 mins easy, 10 mins steady, 10 mins brisk); PM bike (5 mins easy, 20 mins steady, 15 mins brisk, 15 mins steady, 5 mins easy)	AM run (15 mins easy, 15 mins steady); PM bike (5 mins easy, 20 mins steady, 10 mins brisk, 20 mins steady, 5 mins easy)	bike 2 hrs 15 mins easy to steady at 80–90 rpm, straight into run (15 mins brisk, then 5 mins easy)

THURSDAY	FRIDAY	SATURDAY	SUNDAY
AM run (10 mins easy, then 10 x 30 secs hard with 1 min easy after each, then 5 mins easy); PM swim 1,500 m nonstop easy	rest	bike 60 mins easy (include 3 x 1 min at race effort with 4 mins easy after each, and 3 x 30 secs hard with 4.5 mins after each)	sprint-distance triathlon, 10-km running race, or bike time trial (10 to 25 miles)

tackling the Olympic continued

WEEK	MONDAY	TUESDAY	WEDNESDAY	
5	rest	**AM** run 70 mins (50 mins easy, 10 mins steady, 5 mins brisk, 5 mins easy); **PM** swim 4 x 100 m easy with 15 secs rest after each, then 3 x (12 x 25 m pull, then 1 x 200 m hard swim. Take 20 secs rest after each 25 m, and 3 mins after each 200 m, and do every fifth 25 m hard). Finish with 4 x 50 m easy. Do the first set of 25 m as pull with paddles	bike 60 mins easy (include 3 x 5 mins in a big gear, alternating 10 secs very hard with 20 secs easy at 40–60 rpm. Take 5 mins easy between blocks)	
6	rest	**AM** run 80 mins (60 mins easy, 10 mins steady, 5 mins brisk, 5 mins easy); **PM** swim 4 x 100 m easy with 15 secs rest after each, then 3 x (12 x 25 m pull, then 1 x 200 m hard swim. Take 20 secs rest after each 25 m, and 3 mins after each 200 m, and do every fifth 25 m hard). Finish with 4 x 50 m easy. Do the first two sets of 25 m as pull with paddles	bike 60 mins easy (include 2 x 8 mins in a big gear, alternating 10 secs very hard with 20 secs easy at 40–60 rpm. Take 5 mins easy between blocks)	
7	rest	**AM** run 90 mins (70 mins easy, 10 mins steady, 5 mins brisk, 5 mins easy); **PM** swim 4 x 100 m easy with 15 secs rest after each, then 3 x (12 x 25 m pull, then 1 x 200 m hard swim. Take 20 secs rest after each 25 m, and 3 mins after each 200 m, and do every fifth 25 m hard). Finish with 4 x 50 m easy. Do all three sets of 25 m as pull with paddles	bike 60 mins easy (include 2 x 10 mins in a big gear, alternating 10 secs very hard with 20 secs easy at 40–60 rpm. Take 5 mins easy between blocks)	

WEEK	MONDAY	TUESDAY	WEDNESDAY	
8 RECOVERY	rest	**AM** run 60 mins easy; **PM** swim 4 x 100 m easy with 15 secs rest after each, then 3 x (8 x 25 m pull, then 1 x 200 m hard swim. Take 20 secs rest after each 25 m, and 3 mins after each 200 m). Finish with 4 x 50 m easy. No paddles!	bike 60 mins easy at 80–90 rpm (include 8 x 20-sec very hard seated bursts with about 5 mins easy after each)	

Training the standard

Like sprint-distance racing, the key to Olympic-distance performance is threshold speed. However, now that the distances have doubled, you'll also need the basic endurance to push on without pause for the entire duration of your race, and particularly the ability to maintain your best possible run pace after upward of 90 minutes of continuous, subthreshold effort.

THURSDAY	FRIDAY	SATURDAY	SUNDAY
AM run (10 mins easy, then 12 x 90 secs hard with 30 secs walk after each, then 10 mins easy); PM swim 400 m easy with every fourth length backstroke, 15 x 100 m steady with 10 secs rest after each. Finish with 4 x 50 m easy	AM run (10 mins easy, then 12 x 90 secs hard with 30 secs walk after each, then 10 mins easy); PM swim 400 m easy with every fourth length backstroke, 15 x 100 m steady with 10 secs rest after each. Finish with 4 x 50 m easy	swim 400 m easy with every fourth length backstroke, 30 x 50 m steady pull with 10 secs rest after each, and every fifth 50 m hard. Finish with 4 x 50 m easy	bike 2hrs 30 easy to steady at 80–90 rpm, straight into run (15 mins brisk, then 5 mins easy)
AM run (10 mins easy, then 13 x 90 secs hard with 30 secs walk after each, then 10 mins easy); PM swim 400 m easy with every fourth length backstroke, 15 x 100 m steady with 10 secs rest after each. Finish with 4 x 50 m easy	AM run (10 mins easy, 10 mins steady, 10 mins brisk); PM bike (5 mins easy, 20 mins steady, 15 mins brisk, 15 mins steady, 5 mins easy)	swim 400 m easy with every fourth length backstroke, 30 x 50 m steady pull with 10 secs rest after each, and every fourth 50 m hard. Finish with 4 x 50 m easy	bike 2hrs 45 mins easy to steady at 80–90 rpm, straight into run (20 mins brisk, then 5 mins easy)
AM run (10 mins easy, then 14 x 90 secs hard with 30 secs walk after each, then 10 mins easy); PM swim 400 m easy with every fourth length backstroke, 15 x 100 m steady with 10 secs rest after each. Finish with 4 x 50 m easy	AM run (10 mins easy, 10 mins steady, 10 mins brisk); PM bike (5 mins easy, 15 mins steady, 20 mins brisk, 15 mins steady, 5 mins easy)	swim 400 m easy with every fourth length backstroke, 30 x 50 m steady pull with 10 secs rest after each, and every third 50 m hard. Finish with 4 x 50 m easy	bike 3 hrs easy to steady at 80–90 rpm, straight into run (25 mins brisk, then 5 mins easy)

THURSDAY	FRIDAY	SATURDAY	SUNDAY
AM run (10 mins easy, then 10 x 30 secs hard with 1 min easy after each, then 5 mins easy); PM swim 1,500 m nonstop easy	rest	bike 60 mins easy (include 3 x 1 min at race effort with 4 mins easy after each, and 3 x 30 secs hard with 4.5 mins after each)	sprint-distance triathlon

tackling the Olympic continued

WEEK	MONDAY	TUESDAY	WEDNESDAY	
9	rest	**AM** run 90 mins (70 mins easy, 10 mins steady, 5 mins brisk, 5 mins easy); **PM** swim 4 x 100 m easy with 15 secs rest after each, then 3 x (12 x 25 m pull, then 1 x 200 m hard swim. Take 20 secs rest after each 25 m, and 3 mins after each 200 m, and do every fifth 25 m hard). Finish with 4 x 50 m easy. Do all three sets of 25 m as pull with paddles	bike 60 mins easy (include 3 x 5 mins in a big gear, alternating 15 secs very hard with 15 secs easy at 40–60 rpm. Take 5 mins easy between blocks)	
10	rest	**AM** run 90 mins (65 mins easy, 15 mins steady, 5 mins brisk, 5 mins easy); **PM** swim 4 x 100 m easy with 15 secs rest after each, then 3 x (12 x 25 m pull, then 1 x 200 m hard swim. Take 20 secs rest after each 25 m, and 3 mins after each 200 m, and do every fifth 25 m hard). Finish with 4 x 50 m easy. Do all three sets of 25 m as pull with paddles	bike 60 mins easy (include 2 x 8 mins in a big gear, alternating 15 secs very hard with 15 secs easy at 40–60 rpm. Take 5 mins easy between blocks)	
11	rest	**AM** run 90 mins (60 mins easy, 15 mins steady, 10 mins brisk, 5 mins easy); **PM** swim 4 x 100 m easy with 15 secs rest after each, then 3 x (12 x 25 m pull, then 1 x 200 m hard swim. Take 20 secs rest after each 25 m, and 3 mins after each 200 m, and do every fifth 25 m hard). Finish with 4 x 50 m easy. Do all three sets of 25 m as pull with paddles	bike 60 mins easy (include 2 x 10 mins in a big gear, alternating 15 secs very hard with 15 secs easy at 40–60 rpm. Take 5 mins easy between blocks)	
12	rest	run 20 mins easy; swim 4 x 100 m easy with 15 secs rest after each, then 2 x (12 x 25 m pull, then 1 x 200 m hard swim. Take 20 secs rest after each 25 m, and 3 mins after each 200 m, and do every fifth 25 m hard). Finish with 4 x 50 m easy. Do all three sets of 25 m as pull with paddles	bike 60 mins easy (include 3 x 1 min at race effort with 4 mins easy after each, and 3 x 30 secs hard with 4.5 mins after each)	

RACE WEEK

THURSDAY	FRIDAY	SATURDAY	SUNDAY
AM run (10 mins easy, 10 mins steady, 10 mins brisk); **PM** swim 400 m easy with every fourth length backstroke, 10 x 150 m steady with 10 secs rest after each. Finish with 4 x 50 m easy	bike (5 mins easy, 15 mins steady, 20 mins brisk, 15 mins steady, 5 mins easy), straight into run (20 mins brisk, 5 mins walk)	swim 400 m easy with every fourth length backstroke, 30 x 50 m steady pull with paddles, with 10 secs rest after each and every fifth 50 m hard. Finish with 4 x 50 m easy	bike 3 hrs easy to steady at 80–90 rpm, straight into run (25 mins brisk, then 5 mins easy)
AM run (10 mins easy, 10 mins steady, 10 mins brisk); **PM** swim 400 m easy with every fourth length backstroke, 10 x 150 m steady with 10 secs rest after each. Finish with 4 x 50 m easy	bike (5 mins easy, 30 mins steady, 20 mins brisk, 5 mins easy), straight into run (20 mins brisk, 5 mins walk)	swim 400 m easy with every fourth length backstroke, 30 x 50 m steady pull with paddles, with 10 secs rest after each and every fourth 50 m hard. Finish with 4 x 50 m easy	bike 3 hrs easy to steady at 80–90 rpm, straight into run (25 mins brisk, then 5 mins easy)
AM run (10 mins easy, 10 mins steady, 10 mins brisk); **PM** swim 400 m easy with every fourth length backstroke, 10 x 150 m steady with 10 secs rest after each. Finish with 4 x 50 m easy	bike (5 mins easy, 25 mins steady, 25 mins brisk, 5 mins easy), straight into run (20 mins brisk, 5 mins walk)	swim 400 m easy with every fourth length backstroke, 30 x 50 m steady pull with paddles, with 10 secs rest after each and every third 50 m hard. Finish with 4 x 50 m easy	bike 3 hrs easy to steady at 80–90 rpm, straight into run (25 mins brisk, then 5 mins easy)
AM swim 30 x 50 m easy with 15 secs rest after each. Do every fourth 50 m hard; **PM** run 20 mins easy	rest	run 15 mins easy (include 2 x 30 secs brisk effort). Swim 15 mins easy (include 2 x 1 min brisk effort). Bike 30 mins (include 1 x 1min brisk and 1 x 30 secs hard). Spread the sessions throughout the day in the order given	**RACE!**

5

half-Ironman

Sooner or later, almost every triathlete thinks about trying to go a little longer. And while some jump straight off the deep end into the tough, but rewarding, world of Ironman, most step up to middle-distance first. So, if you're thinking of taking that step up, here's a 16-week plan to help you prepare.

WEEK	MONDAY	TUESDAY	WEDNESDAY	
1	**AM** run 60 mins easy; **PM** swim 4 x 100 m easy with 15 secs rest after each, then 3 x (12 x 25 m steady pull with paddles (see page 104), then 1 x 200 m hard swim. Take 20 secs rest after each 25 m, and 3 mins after each 200 m). Finish with 4 x 50 m easy	bike 60 mins (ride easy at 95–100 rpm, but do a 20-sec very hard burst at 115–125 rpm every 5 mins)	rest	

WEEK		MONDAY	TUESDAY	WEDNESDAY	
2		rest	**AM** run 55 mins easy; **PM** swim 4 x 100 m easy with 15 secs rest after each, then 3 x (12 x 25 m steady pull with paddles, then 1 x 200 m hard swim. Take 20 secs rest after each 25 m, and 3 mins after each 200 m). Finish with 4 x 50 m easy. Do every fourth 25 m hard	bike 70 mins (ride easy at 95–100 rpm, but do a 20-sec very hard burst at 115–125 rpm every 5 mins)	
3		rest	**AM** run 70 mins easy; **PM** swim 4 x 100 m easy with 15 secs rest after each, then 3 x (12 x 25 m steady pull with paddles, then 1 x 200 m hard swim. Take 20 secs rest after each 25 m, and 3 mins after each 200 m). Finish with 4 x 50 m easy. Do every third 25 m hard	bike 80 mins (ride easy at 95–100 rpm, but do a 20-sec very hard burst at 115–125 rpm every 5 mins)	
4		rest	**AM** run 65 mins easy; **PM** swim 4 x 100 m easy with 15 secs rest after each, then 3 x (10 x 25 m steady pull, then 1 x 200 m hard swim. Take 20 secs rest after each 25 m, and 3 mins after each 200 m, and do every fifth 25 m hard). Finish with 4 x 50 m easy. No paddles!	swim 2,000 m easy nonstop	

RECOVERY

SETTING THE PACE

To get the pacing right in your Saturday swim, swim the 400 m effort easy and record the time. Try to beat half that time for your 200 m, beat half your 200 m time for the 100 m, and so on.

THURSDAY	FRIDAY	SATURDAY	SUNDAY
AM run (15 mins easy, 3 x 5 mins brisk with 1 min walk after each, then 12 mins easy); **PM** bike 60 mins steady at 80–90 rpm	swim (20 x 100 m steady with 10 secs rest after each. First 4 and last 2 100 m easy, all others at target race pace)	**AM** run 30 mins (10 mins easy, 10 mins steady, 10 mins brisk); **PM** swim 400 m, then 2 x 200 m pull with paddles, then 4 x 100 m swim, then 8 x 50 m pull with paddles, then 16 x 25 m swim. Make each set faster than the one before, and take 15 secs rest between efforts. Finish with 4 x 100 m easy with every fourth length backstroke	bike 2 hrs (include 2 x 15 mins brisk), straight into run 20 mins (5 mins easy, 10 mins brisk, 5 mins easy)

THURSDAY	FRIDAY	SATURDAY	SUNDAY
AM run (15 mins easy, 3 x 6 mins brisk with 1 min walk after each, then 8 mins easy); **PM** bike (5 mins easy at 95–100 rpm, 30 mins steady, 10 mins brisk, 10 mins steady all at 80–90 rpm, then 5 mins easy at 95–100 rpm)	swim (22 x 100 m steady with a 10-sec rest after each. First 4 and last 2 100 m easy, all others at target race pace)	**AM** run 35 mins (15 mins easy, 10 mins steady, 10 mins brisk); **PM** swim 400 m, then 2 x 200 m pull with paddles, then 4 x 100 m swim, then 8 x 50 m pull with paddles, then 16 x 25 m swim. Make each set faster than before, take 15 secs rest between efforts. Finish with 4 x 100 m easy with every fourth length backstroke	bike 2 hrs 30 mins (include 2 x 15 mins brisk), straight into run 20 mins (5 mins easy, 10 mins brisk, 5 mins easy)
AM run (15 mins easy, 3 x 7 mins brisk with 1 min walk after each, then 6 mins easy); **PM** bike (5 mins easy at 95–100 rpm, 25 mins steady, 15 mins brisk, 10 mins steady, all at at 80–90 rpm, then 5 mins easy at 95–100 rpm)	swim (24 x 100 m steady with 10 secs rest after each. First 4 and last 2 100 m easy, all others at target race pace)	**AM** run 40 mins (15 mins easy, 15 mins steady, 10 mins brisk); **PM** swim 400 m, then 2 x 200 m pull with paddles, then 4 x 100 m swim, then 8 x 50 m pull with paddles, then 16 x 25 m swim. Make each set faster than the one before, and take 15 secs rest between efforts. Finish with 4 x 100 m easy with every fourth length backstroke	bike 3 hrs (include 3 x 15 mins brisk), straight into run 20 mins (5 mins easy, 10 mins brisk, 5 mins easy)
AM run 30 mins easy; **PM** bike 60 mins easy at 80–90 rpm (include 8 x 20-sec very hard seated bursts with about 5 mins easy after each)	rest	bike 60 mins easy (include 3 x 1 min at race effort with 4 mins easy after each, and 3 x 30 secs hard with 4.5 mins after each)	**SPRINT RACE**

half-Ironman continued

Training for a half-Ironman

We may call it a "half-Ironman," but even though all the distances other than the swim are more than double that of a standard-distance race, the training for a middle-distance triathlon has more in common with what you'd do for a shorter race. This is partly because—though the race as a whole is long—the

WEEK	MONDAY	TUESDAY	WEDNESDAY	
5	rest	**AM** run 80 mins: **PM** swim (400 m easy with every fourth length backstroke, then 40 x 50 m pull with paddles with 10 secs rest after each. Do every fifth 50 m hard. Finish with 4 x 25 m easy)	bike 70 mins (ride easy at 95–100 rpm, but do a 20-sec very hard burst at 115–125 rpm every 5 mins)	
6	rest	**AM** run 75 mins easy; **PM** swim (400 m easy with every fourth length backstroke, then 40 x 50 m pull with paddles with 10 secs rest after each. Do every fourth 50 m hard. Finish with 4x 25 m easy)	bike 80 mins (ride easy at 95–100 rpm, but do a 20-sec very hard burst at 115–125 rpm every 5 mins)	
7	rest	**AM** run 90 mins easy; **PM** swim (400 m easy with every fourth length backstroke, then 40 x 50 m pull with paddles with 10 secs rest after each. Do every third 50 m hard. Finish with 4 x 25 m easy)	bike 90 mins (ride easy at 95–100 rpm, but do a 20-sec very hard burst at 115–125 rpm every 5 mins)	
8	rest	**AM** run 85 mins easy; **PM** swim 4 x 100 m easy with 15 secs rest after each, then 3 x (10 x 25 m steady pull, then 1 x 200 m hard swim. Take 20 secs rest after each 25 m, and 3 mins after each 200 m, and do every fifth 25 m hard). Finish with 4 x 50 m easy. No paddles!	swim 2,000 m easy nonstop	

RECOVERY

individual distances within a half-Ironman should be reasonably manageable for someone who is used to training for Olympic-distance races, and partly because, as you get to races that last beyond eight or nine hours, the demands on your body and the things that determine your performance change.

THURSDAY	FRIDAY	SATURDAY	SUNDAY
AM run (15 mins easy, 2 x 9 mins brisk with 1 min walk after each, then 10 mins easy); PM bike (5 mins easy at 95–100 rpm, 30 mins steady, 10 mins brisk, 10 mins steady all at 80–90 rpm, then 5 mins easy at 95–100 rpm)	swim (24 x 100 m steady with 10 secs rest after each. First 4 and last 2 100 m easy, all others at target race pace)	AM run 40 mins (15 mins easy, 15 mins steady, 10 mins brisk); PM swim 5 x (400 m steady pull, 4 x 25 m hard paddles only, all with 20 secs rest). Get faster each set	bike 3 hrs (include 3 x 15 mins brisk), straight into run 30 mins (15 mins easy, 10 mins brisk, 5 mins easy)
AM run (15 mins easy, 2 x 10 mins brisk with 1 min walk after each, then 8 mins easy); PM bike (5 mins easy at 95–100 rpm, 25 mins steady, 15 mins brisk, 10 mins steady, all at 80–90 rpm, then 5 mins easy at 95–100 rpm)	swim (26 x 100 m steady with 10 secs rest after each. First 4 and last 2 100 m easy, all others at target race pace)	AM run 45 mins (15 mins easy, 15 mins steady, 15 mins brisk); PM swim 5 x (400 m steady pull, 4 x 25 m hard paddles only, all with 20 secs rest). Get faster each set	bike 3 hrs 30 mins (include 3 x 15 mins brisk), straight into run 30 mins (10 mins easy, 15 mins brisk, 5 mins easy)
AM run (15 mins easy, 2 x 11 mins brisk with 1 min walk after each, then 6 mins easy); PM bike (5 mins easy at 95–100 rpm, 20 mins steady, 20 mins brisk, 10 mins steady, all at 80–90 rpm, then 5 mins easy at 95–100 rpm)	swim (28 x 100 m steady with 10 secs rest after each. First 4 and last 2 100 m easy, all others at target race pace)	AM run 50 mins (20 mins easy, 15 mins steady, 15 mins brisk); PM swim 5 x (400 m steady pull, 4 x 25 m hard paddles only, all with 20 secs rest). Get faster each set	bike 4 hrs (include 4 x 15 mins brisk), straight into run 30 mins (5 mins easy, 20 mins brisk, 5 mins easy)
AM run 30 mins easy; PM bike 60 mins easy at 80–90 rpm (include 8 x 20-sec very hard seated bursts with about 5 mins easy after each)	rest	bike 60 mins easy (include 3 x 1 min at race effort with 4 mins easy after each, and 3 x 30 secs hard with 4.5 mins after each)	Olympic race at target half-Ironman pace OR a sprint tri raced flat out!

half-Ironman continued

Steady pace in these last weeks of race preparation should be identical to your target race effort.

WEEK	MONDAY	TUESDAY	WEDNESDAY	
9	rest	**AM** run 1 hr 40 mins easy; **PM** swim (400 m easy with every fourth length backstroke, then 20 x 100 m steady pull with paddles with 30 secs rest after each. Finish with 4 x 25 m easy)	bike 80 mins (ride easy at 95–100 rpm, but do a 20-sec very hard burst at 115–125 rpm every 5 mins)	
10	rest	**AM** run 1 hr 35 mins; **PM** swim (400 m easy with every fourth length backstroke, then 20 x 100 m steady pull with paddles with 25 secs rest after each. Finish with 4 x 25 m easy)	bike 90 mins (ride easy at 95–100 rpm, but do a 20-sec very hard burst at 115–125 rpm every 5 mins)	
11	rest	**AM** run 1 hr 50 mins; **PM** swim (400 m easy with every fourth length backstroke, then 20 x 100 m steady pull with paddles with 20 secs rest after each. Finish with 4 x 25 m easy)	bike 1 hr 40 mins (ride easy at 95–100 rpm, but do a 20-sec very hard burst at 115–125 rpm every 5 mins)	
12 RECOVERY	rest	**AM** run 1 hr 45 mins easy; **PM** swim 4 x 100 m easy with 15 secs rest after each, then 3 x (10 x 25 m steady pull, then 1 x 200 m hard swim. Take 20 secs rest after each 25 m, and 3 mins after each 200 m, and do every fifth 25 m hard). Finish with 4 x 50 m easy. No paddles!	swim 2,000 m easy nonstop	

AEROBAR RIDING

Try to do as much of your riding as possible on your aerobars. Make a particular effort to use your areobars when doing any brisk, hard, or very hard efforts.

THURSDAY	FRIDAY	SATURDAY	SUNDAY
AM run (20 mins easy, 20 mins brisk, then 5 mins easy); **PM** bike (5 mins easy at 95–100 rpm, 20 mins steady, 20 mins brisk, 10 mins steady, all at 80–90 rpm, then 5 mins easy at 95–100 rpm)	swim (26 x 100 m steady with 10 secs rest after each. First 4 and last 2 100 m easy, all others at target race pace)	run 50 mins (20 mins easy, 15 mins steady, 15 mins brisk), swim (400 m easy with every fourth length backstroke, then 40 x 50 m pull with paddles with 10 secs rest after each. Do every fifth 50 m hard. Finish with 4 x 25 m easy)	bike 4 hrs (include 4 x 15 mins brisk), straight into run 40 mins (15 mins easy, 20 mins brisk, 5 mins easy)
AM run (15 mins easy, 25 mins brisk, then 5 mins easy); **PM** bike (5 mins easy at 95–100 rpm, 25 mins steady, 20 mins brisk, all at 80–90 rpm, then 10 mins easy at 95-100 rpm)	swim (28 x 100 m steady with 10 secs rest after each. First 4 and last 2 100 m easy, all others at target race pace)	run 55 mins (20 mins easy, 20 mins steady, 15 mins brisk), swim (400 m easy with every fourth length backstroke, then 40 x 50 m pull with paddles with 10 secs rest after each. Do every fourth 50 m hard. Finish with 4 x 25 m easy)	bike 4 hrs (include 3 x 20 mins brisk), straight into run 40 mins (10 mins easy, 25 mins brisk, 5 mins easy)
AM run (10 mins easy, 30 mins brisk, then 5 mins easy); **PM** bike (5 mins easy at 95–100 rpm, 30 mins steady, 20 mins brisk all at 80–90 rpm, then 5 mins easy at 95–100 rpm)	swim (30 x 100 m steady with 10 secs rest after each. First 4 and last 2 100 m easy, all others at target race pace)	run 60 mins (20 mins easy, 20 mins steady, 20 mins brisk), swim (400 m easy with every fourth length backstroke, then 40 x 50 m pull with paddles with 10 secs rest after each. Do every third 50 m hard. Finish with 4 x 25 m easy)	bike 4 hrs (include 4 x 20 mins brisk), straight into run 40 mins (5 mins easy, 30 mins brisk, 5 mins easy)
AM run 30 mins easy; **PM** bike 60 mins easy at 80–90 rpm (include 8 x 20-sec very hard seated bursts with about 5 mins easy after each)	rest	bike 60 mins easy (include 3 x 1 min at race effort with 4 mins easy after each, and 3 x 30 secs hard with 4.5 mins after each)	**OLYMPIC RACE** race at target half-Ironman pace

half-Ironman continued

WEEK	MONDAY	TUESDAY	WEDNESDAY	
13	rest	**AM** run 2 hrs; **PM** swim 400 m easy, 2 x 200 m beat half your 400-m time, 4 x 100 m beat half your 200-m time, 8 x 50 m beat half your 100-m time, then 16 x 25 m beat half your 50-m time. Do all efforts as pull, and take 15 secs rest after each	bike 90 mins (ride easy at 95–100 rpm, but do a 20-sec very hard burst at 115–125 rpm every 5 mins)	
14	rest	**AM** run 90 mins easy; **PM** swim 400 m easy, 2 x 200 m beat half your 400-m time, 4 x 100 m beat half your 200-m time, 8 x 50 m beat half your 100-m time, then 16 x 25 m beat half your 50-m time. Do all efforts as pull, and take 15 secs rest after each	bike 90 mins (ride easy at 95–100 rpm, but do a 20-sec very hard burst at 115–125 rpm every 5 mins)	
15	rest	**AM** run 1 hr easy; **PM** swim 400 m easy, 2 x 200 m beat half your 400-m time, 4 x 100 m beat half your 200-m time, 8 x 50 m beat half your 100-m time, then 16 x 25 m beat half your 50-m time. Do all efforts as pull, and take 15 secs rest after each	bike 90 mins (ride easy at 95–100 rpm, but do a 20-sec very hard burst at 115–125 rpm every 5 mins)	
16 *RACE WEEK*	rest	**AM** run 30 mins easy (include 6 x 10 secs fast, light strides spread throughout the run); **PM** swim 4 x 100 m easy with 15 secs rest after each, then 2 x (12 x 25 m steady pull with paddles, then 1 x 200 m hard swim. Take 20 secs rest after each 25 m, and 3 mins after each 200 m, and do every fifth 25 m hard). Finish with 4 x 50 m easy	bike 60 mins easy at 80–90 rpm	

FUEL UP

Use your long rides to experiment with different feeding strategies for race day. If possible, buy some samples of the nutrition that will be available on the course, and try them on a long ride to see how well you cope using them for fuel and hydration.

THURSDAY	FRIDAY	SATURDAY	SUNDAY
bike 60 mins (20 mins easy, 20 mins steady, 20 mins brisk, all at 80–90 rpm), straight into run 30 mins (20 mins brisk, 10 mins easy)	swim (30 x 100 m steady with 10 secs rest after each. First 4 and last 2 100 m easy, all others at target race pace)	AM run 60 mins (20 mins easy, 20 mins steady, 20 mins brisk); PM swim 5 x (400 m steady pull, 4 x 25 m hard paddles only, all with 20 secs rest). Get faster each set	bike 4 hrs (1 hr easy, 90 mins steady, 30 mins brisk, 1 hr easy), straight into run 40 mins (5 mins easy, 30 mins brisk, 5 mins easy)
bike 60 mins (20 mins easy, 20 mins steady, 20 mins brisk, all at 80–90 rpm), straight into run 30 mins (25 mins brisk, 5 mins easy)	swim (30 x 100 m steady with 10 secs rest after each. First 4 and last 2 100 m easy, all others at target race pace)	AM run 60 mins (20 mins easy, 20 mins steady, 20 mins brisk); PM swim 5 x (400 m steady pull, 4 x 25 m hard paddles only, all with 20 secs rest). Get faster each set	bike 3 hrs (30 mins easy, 90 mins steady, 30 mins brisk, 30 mins easy), straight into run 40 mins (5 mins easy, 30 mins brisk, 5 mins easy)
bike 60 mins (20 mins easy, 20 mins steady, 20 mins brisk, all at 80–90 rpm), straight into run 30 mins (30 mins brisk)	AM swim (30 x 100 m steady with 10 secs rest after each. First 4 and last 2 100 m easy, all others at target race pace); PM run 45 mins (15 mins easy, 15 mins steady, 15 mins brisk)	rest	bike 2 hrs (30 mins easy, 60 mins steady, 30 mins brisk), straight into run 20 mins (15 mins brisk, 5 mins easy)
AM swim 20 x 50 m pull at target race pace with 10 secs rest after each. Do every fourth 50 m hard; PM run 30 mins easy (include 6 x 10 secs fast, light strides spread throughout the run)	rest	run 15 mins easy (include 2 x 30 secs brisk effort). Swim 15 mins easy (include 2 x 1 min brisk effort). Bike 30 mins (include 1 x 1min brisk and 1 x 30 secs hard). Spread the sessions throughout the day in the order given	**HALF-IRONMAN** middle-distance race

6 Ironman

Long-distance racing is the ultimate challenge in triathlon—a demanding mix of ultralong distances and the fatigue they bring, refueling difficulties that begin in the swim, and the cumulative pounding of a full marathon to finish. It's also

WEEK	MONDAY	TUESDAY	WEDNESDAY	
1	**AM** run 45 mins easy; **PM** swim 400 m, then 2 x 200 m pull, then 4 x 100 m, then 8 x 50 m pull, then 16 x 25 m. Make each set faster than the one before, and take 15 secs rest between efforts	**AM** run 90 mins easy; **PM** swim 4 x 100 m easy with 15 secs rest after each, then 3 x (12 x 25 m steady pull, then 1 x 200 m hard swim. Take 20 secs rest after each 25 m, and 3 mins after each 200 m). Finish with 4 x 50 m easy	bike 90 mins (ride easy at 95–100 rpm, but with a 20-sec very hard burst at 115–125 rpm every 5 mins)	

WEEK	MONDAY	TUESDAY		WEDNESDAY	
2	rest	**AM** run 45 mins (10 mins easy, 4 x 5 mins brisk with 1 min walk after each, then about 10 mins easy); **PM** swim 400 m, then 2 x 200 m pull, then 4 x 100 m, then 8 x 50 m pull, then 16 x 25 m. Make each set faster than the one before, and take 15 secs rest between efforts		**AM** run 1 hr 45 mins easy; **PM** swim 4 x 100 m easy with 15 secs rest after each, then 3 x (12 x 25 m steady pull, then 1 x 200 m hard. Take 20 secs rest after each 25 m, and 3 mins after each 200 m). Finish with 4 x 50 m easy. Do every fourth 25 m hard and use paddles for the first set of 25 m	
3	rest	**AM** run 45 mins (10 mins easy, 4 x 5 mins brisk with 1 min walk after each, then about 10 mins easy); **PM** swim 400 m, then 2 x 200 m pull, then 4 x 100 m, then 8 x 50 m pull, then 16 x 25 m. Make each set faster than the one before, and take 15 secs rest between efforts		**AM** run 1 hr 40 mins easy; **PM** swim 4 x 100 m easy with 15 secs rest after each, then 3 x (12 x 25 m steady pull, then 1 x 200 m hard. Take 20 secs rest after each 25 m, and 3 mins after each 200 m). Finish with 4 x 50 m easy. Do every fourth 25 m hard, and use paddles for the first two sets of 25 m	
4	rest	**AM** run (10 mins easy, then 10 x 30 secs hard with 1 min easy after each, then 5 mins easy); **PM** swim 400 m, then 2 x 200 m pull, then 4 x 100 m, then 8 x 50 m pull, then 16 x 25 m. Make each set faster than the one before, and take 15 secs rest between efforts		**AM** run 60 mins easy; **PM** swim 4 x 100 m easy with 15 secs rest after each, then 2 x (12 x 25 m steady pull, then 1 x 200 m hard. Take 20 secs rest after each 25 m, and 3 mins after each 200 m). Finish with 4 x 50 m easy. Do every fourth 25 m hard and don't use paddles AT ALL	

RECOVERY

perhaps the most satisfying type of triathlon to complete; so, if you like hard work, and you're looking for a race that'll test you to your true limits, use this 24-week training program and get yourself "iron-ready."

THURSDAY	FRIDAY	SATURDAY	SUNDAY
rest	AM run 45 mins (10 mins easy, 4 x 5 mins brisk with 1 min walk after each, then about 10 mins easy); PM swim 20 x 50 m pull with paddles. Take 10 secs rest after each and do every fourth 50 m hard	bike 2 hrs easy to steady, straight into run (5 mins easy, 10 mins brisk, 5 mins easy)	AM bike 60 miles or 3 hrs (easy to steady, but with 10–15 mins brisk in the middle of each whole hour); PM swim 30 x 100 m with 10 secs rest after each. First 3 and last 2 easy, all others steady

THURSDAY	FRIDAY	SATURDAY	SUNDAY
bike 90 mins (ride easy at 95–100 rpm, but with a 20-sec very hard burst at 115–125 rpm every 5 mins)	AM run 45 mins (10 mins easy, 4 x 5 mins brisk with 1 min walk after each, then about 10 mins easy); PM swim 20 x 50 m pull with paddles. Take 10 secs rest after each and do every fourth 50 m hard	bike 2 hrs easy to steady, straight into run (5 mins easy, 15 mins brisk, 5 mins easy)	AM bike 70 miles or 3 hrs 30 mins (easy to steady, but with 10–15 mins brisk in the middle of each whole hour); PM swim 32 x 100 m with 10 secs rest after each. First 3 and last 2 easy, all others steady
bike 90 mins (ride easy at 95–100 rpm, but with a 20-sec very hard burst at 115–125 rpm every 5 mins)	AM run 50 mins (15 mins easy, 4 x 5 mins brisk with 1 min walk after each, then about 10 mins easy); PM swim 20 x 50 pull with paddles. Take 10 secs rest after each and do every fourth 50 m hard	bike 2 hrs easy to steady, straight into run (10 mins easy, 15 mins brisk, 5 mins easy)	AM bike 80 miles or 4 hrs (easy to steady, but with 10–15 mins brisk in the middle of each whole hour); PM swim 34 x 100 m with 10 secs rest after each. First 3 and last 2 easy, all others steady
bike 60 mins (ride easy at 95–100 rpm, but with a 20-sec very hard burst at 115–125 rpm every 5 mins)	AM run (10 mins easy, then 10 x 30 secs hard with 1 min easy after each, then 5 mins easy); PM swim 4 x 500 m steady pull with 30 secs rest after each	rest	bike 3 hrs easy

Ironman continued

Training the Ironman

The sheer length of a long-distance triathlon dictates a great deal of the training. In addition to simply "making yourself fitter," you'll need to improve your body's fuel efficiency and impact resilience. Oddly, you'll find more interval sessions in this program than others. This is partly because they allow you to break up

WEEK	MONDAY	TUESDAY	WEDNESDAY	
5	rest	**AM** run 50 mins (15 mins easy, 3 x 7 mins brisk with 1 min walk after each, then about 10 mins easy); **PM** swim 400 m, then 2 x 200 m pull, then 4 x 100 m, then 8 x 50 m pull with paddles, then 16 x 25 m. Make each set faster than the one before, and take 15 secs rest between efforts	**AM** run 1 hr 40 mins easy; **PM** swim 4 x 100 m easy with 15 secs rest after each, then 3 x (12 x 25 m steady pull, then 1 x 200 m hard. Take 20 secs rest after each 25 m, and 3 mins after each 200 m). Finish with 4 x 50 m easy. Do every fourth 25 m hard and use paddles for the first set of 25 m	
6	rest	**AM** run 50 mins (15 mins easy, 3 x 7 mins brisk with 1 min walk after each, then about 10 mins easy); **PM** swim 400 m, then 2 x 200 m pull, then 4 x 100 m, then 8 x 50 m pull with paddles, then 16 x 25 m. Make each set faster than the one before, and take 15 secs rest between efforts	**AM** run 1 hr 55 mins easy; **PM** swim 4 x 100 m easy with 15 secs rest after each, then 3 x (12 x 25 m steady pull, then 1 x 200 m hard. Take 20 secs rest after each 25 m, and 3 mins after each 200 m). Finish with 4 x 50 m easy. Do every fourth 25 m hard and use paddles for the first two sets of 25 m	
7	rest	**AM** run 50 mins (15 mins easy, 3 x 7 mins brisk with 1 min walk after each, then about 10 mins easy); **PM** swim 400 m, then 2 x 200 m pull, then 4 x 100 m, then 8 x 50 m pull with paddles, then 16 x 25 m. Make each set faster than the one before, and take 15 secs rest between efforts	**AM** run 1 hr 50 mins easy; **PM** swim 4 x 100 m easy with 15 secs rest after each, then 3 x (12 x 25 m steady pull, then 1 x 200 m hard swim. Take 20 secs rest after each 25 m, and 3 mins after each 200 m). Finish with 4 x 50 m easy. Do every fourth 25 m hard and use paddles for all three sets of 25m	
8	rest	**AM** run (10 mins easy, then 10 x 30 secs hard with 1 min easy after each, then 5 mins easy); **PM** swim 400 m, then 2 x 200 m pull, then 4 x 100 m, then 8 x 50 m pull, then 16 x 25 m. Make each set faster than the one before, and take 15 secs rest between efforts	**AM** run 60 mins easy; **PM** swim 4 x 100 m easy with 15 secs rest after each, then 2 x (12 x 25 m steady pull, then 1 x 200 m hard swim. Take 20 secs rest after each 25 m, and 3 mins after each 200 m). Finish with 4 x 50 m easy. Do every fourth 25 m hard and don't use paddles AT ALL	

RECOVERY

otherwise monotonous training into manageable chunks, but also because the shorter blocks should encourage you to develop and maintain good form for each activity, improving your overall economy for the race and hopefully reducing your risk of fatigue-related breakdown and injury.

THURSDAY	FRIDAY	SATURDAY	SUNDAY
bike 90 mins (ride easy at 95–100 rpm, but with a 20-sec very hard burst at 115–125 rpm every 5 mins)	AM run 50 mins (15 mins easy, 3 x 7 mins brisk with 1 min walk after each, then about 10 mins easy); PM swim 25 x 50 m pull with paddles. Take 10 secs rest after each and do every fourth 50 m hard	bike 2 hrs (including 3 x 10 mins brisk at 80–90 rpm with 5 mins easy after each), straight into run (5 mins easy, 15 mins brisk, 5 mins easy)	AM bike 70 miles or 3 hrs 30 mins (easy to steady, but with 15 mins brisk in the middle of each whole hour); PM swim 32 x 100 m with 10 secs rest after each. First 3 and last 2 easy, all others steady
bike 90 mins (ride easy at 95–100 rpm, but with a 20-sec very hard burst at 115–125 rpm every 5 mins)	AM run 50 mins (15 mins easy, 3 x 7 mins brisk with 1 min walk after each, then about 10 mins easy); PM swim 25 x 50 m pull with paddles. Take 10 secs rest after each and do every fourth 50 m hard	bike 2 hrs (including 3 x 10 mins brisk at 80–90 rpm with 5 mins easy after each), straight into run (5 mins easy, 20 mins brisk, 5 mins easy	AM bike 80 miles or 4 hrs (easy to steady, but with 15 mins brisk in the middle of each whole hour); PM swim 34 x 100 m with 10 secs rest after each. First 3 and last 2 easy, all others steady
bike 90 mins (ride easy at 95–100 rpm, but with a 20-sec very hard burst at 115–125 rpm every 5 mins)	AM run 55 mins (20 mins easy, 3 x 7 mins brisk with 1 min walk after each, then about 10 mins easy); PM swim 25 x 50 m pull with paddles. Take 10 secs rest after each and do every fourth 50 m hard	bike 2 hrs (including 3 x 10 mins brisk at 80–90 rpm with 5 mins easy after each), straight into run (10 mins easy, 20 mins brisk, 5 mins easy)	AM bike 90 miles or 4 hrs 30 mins easy to steady (but with 15 mins brisk in the middle of each whole hour); PM swim 36 x 100 m with 10 secs rest after each. First 3 and last 2 easy, all others steady
bike 60 mins (ride easy at 95–100 rpm, but with a 20-sec very hard burst at 115–125 rpm every 5 mins)	AM run (10 mins easy, then 10 x 30 secs hard with 1 min easy after each, then 5 mins easy); PM swim 5 x 500 m steady pull with 30 secs rest after each	rest	bike 3 hrs easy

Ironman continued

WEEK	MONDAY	TUESDAY	WEDNESDAY
9	rest	**AM** run 55 mins (12 mins easy, 3 x 10 mins brisk with 1 min walk after each, then about 10 mins easy); **PM** swim 400 m, then 2 x 200 m pull with paddles, then 4 x 100 m, then 8 x 50 m pull with paddles, then 16 x 25 m. Make each set faster than the one before, and take 15 secs rest between efforts	**AM** run 1 hr 50 mins easy; **PM** swim 4 x 100 m easy with 15 secs rest after each, then 3 x (12 x 25 m steady pull with paddles, then 1 x 200 m hard swim. Take 20 secs rest after each 25 m, and 3 mins after each 200 m). Finish with 4 x 50 m easy
10	rest	**AM** run 55 mins (12 mins easy, 3 x 10 mins brisk with 1 min walk after each, then about 10 mins easy); **PM** swim 400 m, then 2 x 200 m pull with paddles, then 4 x 100 m, then 8 x 50 m pull with paddles, then 16 x 25 m. Make each set faster than the one before, and take 15 secs rest between efforts	**AM** run 2 hrs 5 mins easy; **PM** swim 4 x 100 m easy with 15 secs rest after each, then 3 x (12 x 25 m steady pull with paddles, then 1 x 200 m hard. Take 20 secs rest after each 25 m, and 3 mins after each 200 m). Finish with 4 x 50 m easy
11	rest	**AM** run 55 mins (12 mins easy, 3 x 10 mins brisk with 1 min walk after each, then about 10 mins easy); **PM** swim 400 m, then 2 x 200 m pull with paddles, then 4 x 100 m, then 8 x 50 m pull with paddles, then 16 x 25 m. Make each set faster than the one before, and take 15 secs rest between efforts	**AM** run 2 hrs easy; **PM** swim 4 x 100 m easy with 15 secs rest after each, then 3 x (12 x 25 m steady pull with paddles, then 1 x 200 m hard. Take 20 secs rest after each 25 m, and 3 mins after each 200 m). Finish with 4 x 50 m easy
12	rest	**AM** run (10 mins easy, then 10 x 30 secs hard with 1 min easy after each, then 5 mins easy); **PM** swim 400 m, then 2 x 200 m pull, then 4 x 100 m, then 8 x 50 m pull, then 16 x 25 m. Make each set faster than the one before, and take 15 secs rest between efforts	**AM** run 60 mins easy; **PM** swim 4 x 100 m easy with 15 secs rest after each, then 2 x (12 x 25 m steady pull, then 1 x 200 m hard. Take 20 secs rest after each 25 m, and 3 mins after each 200 m). Finish with 4 x 50 m easy. Do every fourth 25 m hard, and don't use paddles AT ALL

RECOVERY

RUNNING FOCUS

Keeping your running cadence fast and light is always important, but you should make a particular effort to focus on it during the 30-second efforts in your Sunday evening run.

THURSDAY	FRIDAY	SATURDAY	SUNDAY
bike 90 mins (ride easy at 95–100 rpm, but with a 20-sec very hard burst at 115–125 rpm every 5 mins)	AM run 55 mins (12 mins easy, 3 x 10 mins brisk with 1 min walk after each, then about 10 mins easy); PM swim 30 x 50 m pull with paddles. Take 10 secs rest after each and do every fourth 50 m hard	bike 2 hrs (including 2 x 15 mins brisk at 80–90 rpm with 10 mins easy after each), straight into run (10 mins easy, 10 mins steady, 10 mins brisk)	AM bike 80 miles or 4 hrs (easy to steady, but with 15 mins brisk in the middle of each whole hour); PM swim 34 x 100 m with 10 secs rest after each. First 3 and last 2 easy, all others steady
bike 90 mins (ride easy at 95–100 rpm, but with a 20-sec very hard burst at 115–125 rpm every 5 mins)	AM run 55 mins (12 mins easy, 3 x 10 mins brisk with 1 min walk after each, then about 10 mins easy); PM swim 30 x 50 m pull with paddles. Take 10 secs rest after each and do every fourth 50 m hard	bike 2 hrs (including 2 x 15 mins brisk at 80–90 rpm with 10 mins easy after each), straight into run (10 mins easy, 15 mins steady, 10 mins brisk)	AM bike 90 miles or 4 hrs 30 mins (easy to steady, but with 15 mins brisk in the middle of each whole hour); PM swim 36 x 100 m with 10 secs rest after each. First 3 and last 2 easy, all others steady
bike 90 mins (ride easy at 95–100 rpm, but with a 20-sec very hard burst at 115–125 rpm every 5 mins)	AM run 60 mins (15 mins easy, 3 x 10 mins brisk with 1 min walk after each, then about 12 mins easy); PM swim 30 x 50 m pull with paddles. Take 10 secs rest after each and do every fourth 50 m hard	bike 2 hrs (including 2 x 15 mins brisk at 80–90 rpm with 10 mins easy after each), straight into run (15 mins easy, 15 mins steady, 10 mins brisk)	AM bike 100 miles or 5 hrs (easy to steady, but with 15 mins brisk in the middle of each whole hour); PM swim 38 x 100 m with 10 secs rest after each. First 3 and last 2 easy, all others steady
bike 60 mins (ride easy at 95–100 rpm, but with a 20-sec very hard burst at 115–125 rpm every 5 mins)	AM run (10 mins easy, then 10 x 30 secs hard with 1 min easy after each, then 5 mins easy); PM swim 6 x 500 m steady pull with 30 secs rest after each	rest	bike 3 hrs easy

Ironman continued

WEEK	MONDAY	TUESDAY	WEDNESDAY	
13	rest	**AM** run (10 mins easy, then 14 x 1 min hard with 30 secs walk after each, then 10 mins easy); **PM** swim 400 m, then 2 x 200 m pull with paddles, then 4 x 100 m, then 8 x 50 m pull with paddles, then 16 x 25 m. Make each set faster than the one before, and take 15 secs rest between efforts	**AM** run 2hrs easy; **PM** swim 4 x 100 m easy with 15 secs rest after each, then 3 x (12 x 25 m steady pull with paddles, then 1 x 200 m hard. Take 20 secs rest after each 25 m, and 3 mins after each 200 m). Finish with 4 x 50 m easy. Do every fourth 25 m hard	
14	rest	**AM** run (10 mins easy, then 10 x 90 secs hard with 30 secs walk after each, then 10 mins easy); **PM** swim 400 m, then 2 x 200 m pull with paddles, then 4 x 100 m, then 8 x 50 m pull with paddles, then 16 x 25 m. Make each set faster than the one before, and take 15 secs rest between efforts	**AM** run 2 hrs 15 mins easy; **PM** swim 4 x 100 m easy with 15 secs rest after each, then 3 x (12 x 25 m steady pull with paddles, then 1 x 200 m hard. Take 20 secs rest after each 25 m, and 3 mins after each 200 m). Finish with 4 x 50 m easy. Do every fourth 25 m hard	
15	rest	**AM** run (10 mins easy, then 8 x 2 mins hard with 30 secs walk after each, then10 mins easy); **PM** swim 400 m, then 2 x 200 m pull with paddles, then 4 x 100 m, then 8 x 50 m pull with paddles, then 16 x 25 m. Make each set faster than the one before, and take 15 secs rest between efforts	**AM** run 2 hrs 10 mins easy; **PM** swim 4 x 100 m easy with 15 secs rest after each, then 3 x (12 x 25 m steady pull with paddles, then 1 x 200 m hard. Take 20 secs rest after each 25 m, and 3 mins after each 200 m). Finish with 4 x 50 m easy. Do every fourth 25 m hard	

	MONDAY	TUESDAY	WEDNESDAY	
RECOVERY **16**	rest	**AM** run (10 mins easy, then 10 x 30 secs hard with 1 min easy after each, then 5 mins easy); **PM** swim 4 x 100 m easy with 15 secs rest after each, then 2 x (12 x 25 m steady pull, then 1 x 200 m hard. Take 20 secs rest after each 25 m, and 3 mins after each 200 m). Finish with 4 x 50 m easy. Do every fourth 25 m hard	swim 7 x 500 m steady pull with 30 secs rest after each	

KEEP THE PACE

Swim all Sunday's steady 100 m at your target race pace, keeping the same pace from start to finish.

THURSDAY	FRIDAY	SATURDAY	SUNDAY
bike 90 mins (ride easy at 95–100 rpm, but with a 20-sec very hard burst at 115–125 rpm every 5 mins)	**AM** run 60 mins (15 mins easy, 3 x 10 mins brisk with 1 min walk after each, then about 12 mins easy); **PM** swim 30 x 50 m pull with paddles. Take 10 secs rest after each and do every fourth 50 m hard	bike 2 hrs (including 4 x 5 mins, alternating 10 secs very hard with 20 secs easy. Take at least 5 mins easy between blocks), run (10 mins easy, 15 mins steady, 10 mins brisk)	**AM** bike 90 miles or 4 hrs 30 mins (easy to steady, but with 15 mins brisk in the middle of each whole hour); **PM** swim 36 x 100 m with 10 secs rest after each. First 3 and last 2 easy, all others steady
bike 90 mins (ride easy at 95–100 rpm, but with a 20-sec very hard burst at 115–125 rpm every 5 mins)	**AM** run 60 mins (15 mins easy, 3 x 10 mins brisk with 1 min walk after each, then about 12 mins easy); **PM** swim 30 x 50 m pull with paddles. Take 10 secs rest after each and do every fourth 50 m hard	bike 2 hrs (including 4 x 5 mins, alternating 20 secs very hard with 40 secs easy. Take at least 5 mins easy between blocks), run (10 mins easy, 15 mins steady, 15 mins brisk)	**AM** bike 100 miles or 5 hrs (easy to steady, but with 15 mins brisk in the middle of each whole hour); **PM** swim 38 x 100 m with 10 secs rest after each. First 3 and last 2 easy, all others steady
bike 90 mins (ride easy at 95–100 rpm, but with a 20-sec very hard burst at 115–125 rpm every 5 mins)	**AM** run 60 mins (15 mins easy, 3 x 10 mins brisk with 1 min walk after each, then about 12 mins easy); **PM** swim 30 x 50 m pull with paddles. Take 10 secs rest after each and do every fourth 50 m hard	bike 2 hrs (including 4 x 5 mins, alternating 30 secs very hard with 30 secs easy. Take at least 5 mins easy between blocks), run (15 mins easy, 15 mins steady, 15 mins brisk)	**AM** bike 110 miles or 5 hrs 30 mins (easy to steady, but with 15 mins brisk in the middle of each whole hour); **PM** swim 40 x 100 m with 10 secs rest after each. First 3 and last 2 easy, all others steady

THURSDAY	FRIDAY	SATURDAY	SUNDAY
bike 60 mins (ride easy at 95–100 rpm, but with a 20-sec very hard burst at 115–125 rpm every 5 mins), straight into run (15 mins brisk, 5 mins easy)	rest	bike 60 mins easy (include 3 x 1 min at race effort with 4 mins easy after each, and 3 x 30 secs hard with 4.5 mins after each)	race a half-Ironman

Ironman continued

WEEK	MONDAY	TUESDAY	WEDNESDAY	
17	rest	**AM** run 30 mins (10 mins easy, 10 mins brisk, 10 mins easy); **PM** bike 90 mins (including 2 x 15 mins brisk at 80–90 rpm)	**AM** bike 90 mins (including 4 x 5 mins alternating 10 secs very hard with 20 secs easy. Take at least 5 mins easy between blocks); **PM** swim 20 x 200 m with 10 secs rest after each. First 3 and last 2 easy, all others steady	
18	rest	**AM** run 60 mins (20 mins easy, 20 mins brisk, 20 mins easy); **PM** bike 90 mins (including 2 x 15 mins brisk at 80–90 rpm)	**AM** bike 90 mins (including 4 x 5 mins, alternating 10 secs very hard with 20 secs easy. Take at least 5 mins easy between blocks); **PM** swim 20 x 200 m with 10 secs rest after each. First 3 and last 2 easy, all others steady	
19	rest	**AM** run 60 mins (20 mins easy, 20 mins brisk, 20 mins easy); **PM** bike 90 mins (including 2 x 15 mins brisk at 80–90 rpm)	**AM** bike 90 mins (including 4 x 5 mins, alternating 10 secs very hard with 20 secs easy. Take at least 5 mins easy between blocks); **PM** swim 20 x 200 m with 10 secs rest after each. First 3 and last 2 easy, all others steady	
20 RECOVERY	rest	**AM** run (10 mins easy, then 10 x 30 secs hard with 1 min easy, then 5 mins easy); **PM** swim 4 x 100 m easy with 15 secs rest after each, then 2 x (12 x 25 m steady pull, then 1 x 200 m hard. Take 20 secs rest after each 25 m, and 3 mins after each 200 m). Finish with 4 x 50 m easy. Do every fourth 25 m hard. Do not use paddles AT ALL	8 x 500 m steady pull with 30 secs rest after each	

THURSDAY	FRIDAY	SATURDAY	SUNDAY
AM run 2 hrs 15 mins easy; PM swim 4 x 100 m easy with 15 secs rest after each, then 3 x (12 x 25 m steady pull with paddles, then 1 x 200 m hard. Take 20 secs rest after each 25 m, and 3 mins after each 200 m). Finish with 4 x 50 m easy. Do every third 25 m hard	rest	AM swim 400 m, then 2 x 200 m pull with paddles, then 4 x 100 m, then 8 x 50 m pull with paddles, then 16 x 25 m. Each set faster than before, take 15 secs rest between; PM bike 2 hrs (including 2 x 15 mins brisk at 80–90 rpm with 10 mins easy after), straight into run (15 mins easy, 15 mins steady, 15 mins brisk)	AM bike 120 miles or 6 hrs (easy to steady, but with 15 mins brisk in the middle of each whole hour); PM run (10 mins easy, then 10 x 30 secs hard with 1 min easy after each, then 5 mins easy)
AM run 2hrs 30 mins easy; PM swim 4 x 100 m easy with 15 secs rest after each, then 3 x (12 x 25 m steady pull with paddles, then 1 x 200 m hard. Take 20 secs rest after each 25 m, and 3 mins after each 200 m). Finish with 4 x 50 m easy. Do every third 25 m hard	rest	AM swim 400 m, then 2 x 200 m pull with paddles, then 4 x 100 m, then 8 x 50 m pull with paddles, then 16 x 25 m. Each set faster than before, 15 secs rest between; PM bike 3 hrs (three times through 30 mins easy, 20 mins steady, 10 mins brisk)	bike 4 hrs (twice through 60 mins easy, 40 mins steady, 20 mins brisk), straight into run 60 mins steady
AM run 2hrs 20 mins easy; PM swim 4 x 100 m easy with 15 secs rest after each, then 3 x (12 x 25 m steady pull with paddles, then 1 x 200 m hard. Take 20 secs rest after each 25 m, and 3 mins after each 200 m). Finish with 4 x 50 m easy. Do every third 25 m hard	rest	AM swim 400 m, then 2 x 200 m pull with paddles, then 4 x 100 m, then 8 x 50 m pull with paddles, then 16 x 25 m. Each set faster than before, take 15 secs rest between efforts; PM bike 3 hrs (three times through 30 mins easy, 20 mins steady, 10 mins brisk)	bike 4 hrs (twice through 60 mins easy, 40 mins steady, 20 mins brisk), straight into run 75 mins steady
bike 60 mins (ride easy at 95–100 rpm, but with a 20-sec very hard burst at 115–125 rpm every 5 mins), straight into run (15 mins brisk, 5 mins easy)	rest	bike 60 mins easy (include 3 x 1 min hard with 4 mins easy after each, and 3 x 30 secs hard with 4.5 mins after each)	Do a half-Ironman, but do it at target Ironman race pace

Ironman continued

WEEK	MONDAY	TUESDAY	WEDNESDAY	
21	rest	bike 60 mins (ride easy at 95–100 rpm, but with a 20-sec very hard burst at 115–125 rpm every 5 mins)	**AM** run (10 mins easy, then 10 x 30 secs hard with 1 min easy after each, then 5 mins easy); **PM** bike 90 mins (including 4 x 5 mins, alternating 30 secs very hard with 30 secs easy. Take at least 5 mins easy between blocks)	
22	rest	**AM** run 60 mins (20 mins easy, 20 mins brisk, 20 mins easy); **PM** bike 90 mins (including 4 x 5 mins, alternating 30 secs very hard with 30 secs easy. Take at least 5 mins easy between blocks)	swim 4 x 100 m easy with 15 secs rest after each, then 3 x (12 x 25 m steady pull with paddles, then 1 x 200 m hard. Take 20 secs rest after each 25 m, and 3 mins after each 200 m). Finish with 4 x 50 m easy. Do every fourth 25 m hard	
23	rest	**AM** run 60 mins (20 mins easy, 20 mins steady, 20 mins brisk); **PM** bike 90 mins (including 4 x 5 mins, alternating 30 secs very hard with 30 secs easy. Take at least 5 mins easy between blocks)	swim 4 x 100 m easy with 15 secs rest after each, then 2 x (12 x 25 m steady pull with paddles, then 1 x 200 m hard. Take 20 secs rest after each 25 m, and 3 mins after each 200 m). Finish with 4 x 50 m easy. Do every third 25 m hard	
24 RACE WEEK	rest	**AM** run 30 mins easy (include 6 x 10 secs fast, light strides spread throughout the run); **PM** swim 20 x 50 m steady pull with 10 secs rest after each. Do every fourth 50 m hard	bike 60 mins easy (include 3 x 1 min at race effort with 4 mins easy after each, and 3 x 30 secs hard with 4.5 mins after each)	

THURSDAY	FRIDAY	SATURDAY	SUNDAY
swim 20 x 200 m with 10 secs rest after each. First 3 and last 2 easy, all others steady	run 2hrs 30 easy	AM swim 4 x 100 m easy with 15 secs rest after each, then 3 x (12 x 25 m steady pull with paddles, then 1 x 200 m hard. Take 20 secs rest after each 25 m, and 3 mins after each 200 m). Finish with 4 x 50 m easy. Do every third 25 m hard; PM bike 3 hrs (three times through 30 mins easy, 20 mins steady, 10 mins brisk)	bike 4 hrs 30 mins (twice through 75 mins easy, 40 mins steady, 20 mins brisk), straight into run (60 mins steady)
run 2 hrs easy	rest	AM swim 400 m, then 2 x 200 m pull with paddles, then 4 x 100 m, then 8 x 50 m pull with paddles, then 16 x 25 m. Make each set faster than the one before, and take 15 secs rest between efforts; PM bike 3 hrs (three times through 30 mins easy, 20 mins steady, 10 mins brisk)	bike 4 hrs 30 mins (twice through 75 mins easy, 40 mins steady, 20 mins brisk), straight into run (60 mins steady)
AM run (10 mins easy, then 10 x 30 secs hard with 1 min easy after each, then 5 mins easy); PM swim 20 x 200 m with 10 secs rest after each. First 3 and last 2 easy, all others steady	rest	bike 60 mins easy (include 3 x 1 min hard with 4 mins easy after each, and 3 x 30 secs hard with 4.5 mins after each)	sprint-distance triathlon, but done at target race effort
AM run 30 mins easy (include 6 x 10 secs fast, light strides spread throughout the run); PM swim 20 x 50 m steady pull with 10 secs rest after each. Do every fifth 50 m hard	rest	run 15 mins easy (include 2 x 30 secs brisk efforts). Swim 15 mins easy (include 2 x 1 min brisk efforts). Bike 30 mins (include 1 x 1 min brisk and 1 x 30 secs hard). Spread the sessions throughout the day in the order given	**IRONMAN!**

swim training for triathlon

The swim sessions in the schedules are designed to develop three things: your triathlon-specific swimming fitness, muscular endurance, and overall motor skills. Here are some of the key sessions you'll find:

Short rep sets
Swimming many short efforts (25–100 meters) at or around your target race pace will develop your ability to swim aerobically, while the short rest after each effort should help you maintain good technique for longer.

Pull sets
Placing a pull buoy between your thighs lifts your body into a better position in the water and forces you to develop a better catch and pull. Always use an ankle band with your pull buoy so that you don't cheat by kicking.

Paddle sets
Using small paddles (provided you don't have a history of shoulder problems) with your pull buoy increases the amount of water you can catch with each stroke. This increases the load on your arm, shoulder, and back, and also tends to force you to develop a more effective catch.

Build swims
Increasing the pace as you go through a session trains your body to swim well when tired, a skill that's important for middle and long distances, where even the faster swimmers are in the water for half an hour or more.

SKILLS AND DRILLS
There's very little mention of swimming technique and drill in the schedules. Yes, they can help improve your stroke technique, but their benefit is often exaggerated, and, too often, drills are used as a substitute for real training. Different problems require different solutions, and so the best coaches will only give you swim drills after watching you swim.

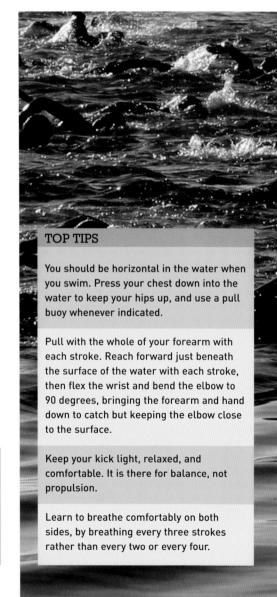

TOP TIPS

You should be horizontal in the water when you swim. Press your chest down into the water to keep your hips up, and use a pull buoy whenever indicated.

Pull with the whole of your forearm with each stroke. Reach forward just beneath the surface of the water with each stroke, then flex the wrist and bend the elbow to 90 degrees, bringing the forearm and hand down to catch but keeping the elbow close to the surface.

Keep your kick light, relaxed, and comfortable. It is there for balance, not propulsion.

Learn to breathe comfortably on both sides, by breathing every three strokes rather than every two or every four.

RACE-DAY SWIM SKILLS

If your race begins with an open-water swim, it will be worth your while perfecting the following four skills:

Surf starts: This one is hard to practice in a pool, but if you are able to do any sea or lake swimming, find a beach and practice running down into the water until it is knee deep, and then diving into the oncoming waves. Keep your knees up and run in fast to build momentum for that first dive into the incoming waves. Expect to feel the beach under your hands as you dive, and grab it and use it to "pull" yourself forward and up through the water to start swimming.

Deep-water starts: Learning to start from floating is simple, particularly if you're using a wetsuit. Simply float upright, kicking gently and facing the direction of the start. To get underway, kick hard and start swimming normally to bring yourself horizontal. Don't dolphin dive, as this can result in other people swimming over the top of you. Practice by starting all of your reps in a session in the deep water of your pool and without pushing off from the wall to start.

Sighting: Open-water swims are notorious for people going wildly off course, so being able to "sight" for the next buoy or landmark is vital. After you turn your head to breathe, keep your head up slightly and let your face turn to the front as your arm comes over for the next stroke. Don't exaggerate the head lift, though; your goggles should be just above the surface of the water.

Turning at buoys: As you approach the buoy marking the turn, switch to breathing every two strokes. Breathe only to the side that you're going to turn toward at the marker, and shorten your stroke so that you can take the turn as close to the buoy as possible. Don't be afraid to cut across other swimmers, and increase your pace slightly entering and leaving the turn. It is a race after all!

bike and run training for triathlon

Cycling is the discipline that underpins your triathlon performance. It's what you'll spend the largest single part of the race doing, and it's the easiest and quickest sport in which to improve your overall endurance and aerobic fitness. It's also the easiest place to find "free speed," from choosing the right riding position and gear to push, and by mastering a few simple skills.

TOP TIPS

Train yourself to ride with a cadence that is slightly slower than your running stride rate (usually somewhere between 80 and 90 rpm).

Use your gears a lot to keep your cadence the same despite the terrain.

Save energy by riding in a nice compact position. Make an effort to get comfortable and confident riding on your aerobars and using your race bike, and try to avoid standing on the pedals on anything other than the steepest hills.

CORNERS, CLIMBS, AND DESCENTS

How to ... corner: Enter the corner from the center of the road, and cut across so that you are close to the curb at the apex of the turn. Pedal smoothly until you're about to enter the corner, then straighten your outside leg, press that foot down into the pedal, and lean your bike into the turn. Make sure you corner with your hands covering your brakes, not on the aerobars, and always look through the corner to where you want to end up. To keep your bike stable, press the knee of your bent leg up into the top tube of your bike. Don't use your brakes once you've entered the corner unless you have no other choice.

How to ... climb: The key to climbing is knowing your limits. Stay in the saddle as much as possible, gradually shift down through the gears to keep your cadence steady, and don't push more than "five percent" harder than you'd be pushing on the flat. If the climb is long or steep, come out of your aerobars and sit up to open your chest, and shift your weight back on the saddle. If you feel you want to stand up, do so, but don't attack, just "dance" on the pedals, swaying your body and bike gently from side to side.

How to ... descend: Shift your weight toward the back of your saddle and move your hands to beside your brakes. Once you've worked through your gears and are up to speed, stop pedaling and coast, turning your legs around gently to keep your muscles loose. Focus your attention along the road well ahead of you, watching for corners, potholes, and changes in gradient. If you need to brake to get through a corner, do so gently and long before you reach the corner itself. Above all else, relax.

You'll end up using all of these skills during training rides, but actively seek out routes that help you practice.

Run training

Running well in a triathlon is built on three things: the aerobic fitness to work hard for the entire race, the durability not to break down under the load of running on legs that are already tired from cycling, and the motor skills to keep you running with fast, light strides despite your tight muscles. It's not complicated: the fitness is built up through regular blocks of brisk, subthreshold work; the durability comes from frequent runs and carefully built progressions of long runs; and the motor skills come from focusing your attention on running with a fast, light, relaxed stride day after day, run after run.

TOP TIPS

Relaxation is important no matter how hard you're working. Try to keep your shoulders back and down, your jaw loose, and your hands relaxed as you run.

Try to keep your stride rate up above 90 footfalls per foot per minute on every run you do. The faster you go, the more footfalls per minute your should be doing. It'll feel odd at first, but stick with it. You'll run better off the bike if you do.

Don't flail. Your arms should be slightly bent and swing naturally in time with your legs without crossing in front of your body. There's no need to "pump" unless you're sprinting for the line.

RUNNING OFF THE BIKE

The ability to get off your bike and run fast right away is a key skill for triathlon, and it's one that you need to practice carefully. Try to make the switch from bike to run as "racelike" as reasonably possible. Get home, get off the bike, grab your running shoes, slip them on, and head straight back out. If you're worried about running out of energy or needing a drink, make sure you stay fully fueled during your ride, and perhaps carry an energy gel as you run. Don't be tempted to do all your runs off the bike, though. The injury risk from too much of this training can be quite high, so only run like this when the schedules tell you to.

triathlete's diary

Recording the details of your training sessions and competitions can prove invaluable in helping you to improve on your performances. You will discover when you were performing at your best, what you ate and drank before and during your training sessions or race, and what the conditions were. You will be able to chart your progress as you work through the training schedules, and see the benefits as you build your fitness and strength.

WEEK 1

DATE

OBJECTIVES

MONDAY

SWIM

1

TIME/DISTANCE	COMMENTS

2

TIME/DISTANCE	COMMENTS

CYCLE

1

TIME/DISTANCE	COMMENTS

2

TIME/DISTANCE	COMMENTS

RUN

1

TIME/DISTANCE	COMMENTS

2

TIME/DISTANCE	COMMENTS

WEATHER CONDITIONS

HOW DO YOU FEEL

BEFORE TRAINING

AFTER TRAINING

TUESDAY

SWIM

1

TIME/DISTANCE	COMMENTS

2

TIME/DISTANCE	COMMENTS

CYCLE

1

TIME/DISTANCE	COMMENTS

2

TIME/DISTANCE	COMMENTS

RUN

1

TIME/DISTANCE	COMMENTS

2

TIME/DISTANCE	COMMENTS

WEATHER CONDITIONS

HOW DO YOU FEEL

BEFORE TRAINING

AFTER TRAINING

WEDNESDAY

SWIM

1

TIME/DISTANCE	COMMENTS

2

TIME/DISTANCE	COMMENTS

CYCLE

1

TIME/DISTANCE	COMMENTS

2

TIME/DISTANCE	COMMENTS

RUN

1

TIME/DISTANCE	COMMENTS

2

TIME/DISTANCE	COMMENTS

WEATHER CONDITIONS

HOW DO YOU FEEL
BEFORE TRAINING

AFTER TRAINING

THURSDAY

SWIM

1

TIME/DISTANCE	COMMENTS

2

TIME/DISTANCE	COMMENTS

CYCLE

1

TIME/DISTANCE	COMMENTS

2

TIME/DISTANCE	COMMENTS

RUN

1

TIME/DISTANCE	COMMENTS

2

TIME/DISTANCE	COMMENTS

WEATHER CONDITIONS

HOW DO YOU FEEL
BEFORE TRAINING

AFTER TRAINING

comments

Are you regular?

Keep your training regular. If you stop for two weeks, then you will lose the benefits of the work you have done so far. Make time for training, and make it part of your routine, but avoid letting it take over your life.

How much do I need to drink?

Don't wait until a competition to start hydrating yourself adequately. Drink regularly and don't rely on thirst to govern your fluid intake. By the time you get thirsty, it is probably too late, and you are already in the early stages of dehydration.

comments

FRIDAY

SWIM

1

TIME/DISTANCE	COMMENTS

2

TIME/DISTANCE	COMMENTS

CYCLE

1

TIME/DISTANCE	COMMENTS

2

TIME/DISTANCE	COMMENTS

RUN

1

TIME/DISTANCE	COMMENTS

2

TIME/DISTANCE	COMMENTS

WEATHER CONDITIONS

HOW DO YOU FEEL
BEFORE TRAINING

AFTER TRAINING

SATURDAY

SWIM

1

TIME/DISTANCE	COMMENTS

2

TIME/DISTANCE	COMMENTS

CYCLE

1

TIME/DISTANCE	COMMENTS

2

TIME/DISTANCE	COMMENTS

RUN

1

TIME/DISTANCE	COMMENTS

2

TIME/DISTANCE	COMMENTS

WEATHER CONDITIONS

HOW DO YOU FEEL
BEFORE TRAINING

AFTER TRAINING

SUNDAY

SWIM

1

TIME/DISTANCE	COMMENTS

2

TIME/DISTANCE	COMMENTS

CYCLE

1

TIME/DISTANCE	COMMENTS

2

TIME/DISTANCE	COMMENTS

RUN

1

TIME/DISTANCE	COMMENTS

2

TIME/DISTANCE	COMMENTS

WEATHER CONDITIONS

HOW DO YOU FEEL

BEFORE TRAINING

AFTER TRAINING

comments

DATE

GOALS MET

GOALS EXCEEDED

NEXT WEEK

SWIMMING NOTES

CYCLING NOTES

RUNNING NOTES

REFUELING NOTES

WEEK 2

OBJECTIVES

_____

_____

_____

DATE

MONDAY

SWIM

1

TIME/DISTANCE	COMMENTS

2

TIME/DISTANCE	COMMENTS

CYCLE

1

TIME/DISTANCE	COMMENTS

2

TIME/DISTANCE	COMMENTS

RUN

1

TIME/DISTANCE	COMMENTS

2

TIME/DISTANCE	COMMENTS

WEATHER CONDITIONS

HOW DO YOU FEEL

BEFORE TRAINING

AFTER TRAINING

TUESDAY

SWIM

1

TIME/DISTANCE	COMMENTS

2

TIME/DISTANCE	COMMENTS

CYCLE

1

TIME/DISTANCE	COMMENTS

2

TIME/DISTANCE	COMMENTS

RUN

1

TIME/DISTANCE	COMMENTS

2

TIME/DISTANCE	COMMENTS

WEATHER CONDITIONS

HOW DO YOU FEEL

BEFORE TRAINING

AFTER TRAINING

WEDNESDAY

SWIM

1

TIME/DISTANCE	COMMENTS

2

TIME/DISTANCE	COMMENTS

CYCLE

1

TIME/DISTANCE	COMMENTS

2

TIME/DISTANCE	COMMENTS

RUN

1

TIME/DISTANCE	COMMENTS

2

TIME/DISTANCE	COMMENTS

WEATHER CONDITIONS

HOW DO YOU FEEL
BEFORE TRAINING

AFTER TRAINING

THURSDAY

SWIM

1

TIME/DISTANCE	COMMENTS

2

TIME/DISTANCE	COMMENTS

CYCLE

1

TIME/DISTANCE	COMMENTS

2

TIME/DISTANCE	COMMENTS

RUN

1

TIME/DISTANCE	COMMENTS

2

TIME/DISTANCE	COMMENTS

WEATHER CONDITIONS

HOW DO YOU FEEL
BEFORE TRAINING

AFTER TRAINING

comments

Extra bounce

As you are running several times a week, you will need to replace your running shoes every five months, at the very least. Check out the latest developments and try a new brand to see if you can add extra bounce to your running!

Be specific

Make sure that your training is geared toward the event you are training for. Don't run mile after mile for a sprint triathlon. Ensure that each session has an aim, whether it be endurance, run speed, or track session.

comments

FRIDAY

SWIM

1

TIME/DISTANCE	COMMENTS

2

TIME/DISTANCE	COMMENTS

CYCLE

1

TIME/DISTANCE	COMMENTS

2

TIME/DISTANCE	COMMENTS

RUN

1

TIME/DISTANCE	COMMENTS

2

TIME/DISTANCE	COMMENTS

WEATHER CONDITIONS

HOW DO YOU FEEL

BEFORE TRAINING

AFTER TRAINING

SATURDAY

SWIM

1

TIME/DISTANCE	COMMENTS

2

TIME/DISTANCE	COMMENTS

CYCLE

1

TIME/DISTANCE	COMMENTS

2

TIME/DISTANCE	COMMENTS

RUN

1

TIME/DISTANCE	COMMENTS

2

TIME/DISTANCE	COMMENTS

WEATHER CONDITIONS

HOW DO YOU FEEL

BEFORE TRAINING

AFTER TRAINING

SUNDAY

SWIM

1

TIME/DISTANCE	COMMENTS

2

TIME/DISTANCE	COMMENTS

CYCLE

1

TIME/DISTANCE	COMMENTS

2

TIME/DISTANCE	COMMENTS

RUN

1

TIME/DISTANCE	COMMENTS

2

TIME/DISTANCE	COMMENTS

WEATHER CONDITIONS

HOW DO YOU FEEL

BEFORE TRAINING

AFTER TRAINING

comments

DATE

GOALS MET

GOALS EXCEEDED

NEXT WEEK

SWIMMING NOTES

CYCLING NOTES

RUNNING NOTES

REFUELING NOTES

WEEK 3

DATE

OBJECTIVES

_____
_____
_____

MONDAY

SWIM

1

TIME/DISTANCE	COMMENTS

2

TIME/DISTANCE	COMMENTS

CYCLE

1

TIME/DISTANCE	COMMENTS

2

TIME/DISTANCE	COMMENTS

RUN

1

TIME/DISTANCE	COMMENTS

2

TIME/DISTANCE	COMMENTS

WEATHER CONDITIONS

HOW DO YOU FEEL

BEFORE TRAINING

AFTER TRAINING

TUESDAY

SWIM

1

TIME/DISTANCE	COMMENTS

2

TIME/DISTANCE	COMMENTS

CYCLE

1

TIME/DISTANCE	COMMENTS

2

TIME/DISTANCE	COMMENTS

RUN

1

TIME/DISTANCE	COMMENTS

2

TIME/DISTANCE	COMMENTS

WEATHER CONDITIONS

HOW DO YOU FEEL

BEFORE TRAINING

AFTER TRAINING

WEDNESDAY

SWIM

1

TIME/DISTANCE	COMMENTS

2

TIME/DISTANCE	COMMENTS

CYCLE

1

TIME/DISTANCE	COMMENTS

2

TIME/DISTANCE	COMMENTS

RUN

1

TIME/DISTANCE	COMMENTS

2

TIME/DISTANCE	COMMENTS

WEATHER CONDITIONS

HOW DO YOU FEEL

BEFORE TRAINING

AFTER TRAINING

THURSDAY

SWIM

1

TIME/DISTANCE	COMMENTS

2

TIME/DISTANCE	COMMENTS

CYCLE

1

TIME/DISTANCE	COMMENTS

2

TIME/DISTANCE	COMMENTS

RUN

1

TIME/DISTANCE	COMMENTS

2

TIME/DISTANCE	COMMENTS

WEATHER CONDITIONS

HOW DO YOU FEEL

BEFORE TRAINING

AFTER TRAINING

comments

Brick workouts

Your legs need to be used to the sensation of running off the bike. A brick workout is when you do two or more workouts, one after the other. For instance, going for a ride, then doing a run session right after.

Keep it exciting

Keep your training varied to keep motivation high. Train with new partners, do different runs, track sessions, hill sprints, fartlek, off road, treadmill—anything that will keep your mind and body working.

comments

FRIDAY	
SWIM	

1

TIME/DISTANCE	COMMENTS

2

TIME/DISTANCE	COMMENTS

CYCLE

1

TIME/DISTANCE	COMMENTS

2

TIME/DISTANCE	COMMENTS

RUN

1

TIME/DISTANCE	COMMENTS

2

TIME/DISTANCE	COMMENTS

WEATHER CONDITIONS

HOW DO YOU FEEL
BEFORE TRAINING

AFTER TRAINING

SATURDAY	
SWIM	

1

TIME/DISTANCE	COMMENTS

2

TIME/DISTANCE	COMMENTS

CYCLE

1

TIME/DISTANCE	COMMENTS

2

TIME/DISTANCE	COMMENTS

RUN

1

TIME/DISTANCE	COMMENTS

2

TIME/DISTANCE	COMMENTS

WEATHER CONDITIONS

HOW DO YOU FEEL
BEFORE TRAINING

AFTER TRAINING

SUNDAY

SWIM

1

TIME/DISTANCE	COMMENTS

2

TIME/DISTANCE	COMMENTS

CYCLE

1

TIME/DISTANCE	COMMENTS

2

TIME/DISTANCE	COMMENTS

RUN

1

TIME/DISTANCE	COMMENTS

2

TIME/DISTANCE	COMMENTS

WEATHER CONDITIONS

HOW DO YOU FEEL

BEFORE TRAINING

AFTER TRAINING

comments

DATE

GOALS MET

GOALS EXCEEDED

NEXT WEEK

SWIMMING NOTES

CYCLING NOTES

RUNNING NOTES

REFUELING NOTES

WEEK 4

DATE

OBJECTIVES

_____
_____
_____

MONDAY

SWIM

1

TIME/DISTANCE	COMMENTS

2

TIME/DISTANCE	COMMENTS

CYCLE

1

TIME/DISTANCE	COMMENTS

2

TIME/DISTANCE	COMMENTS

RUN

1

TIME/DISTANCE	COMMENTS

2

TIME/DISTANCE	COMMENTS

WEATHER CONDITIONS

HOW DO YOU FEEL

BEFORE TRAINING

AFTER TRAINING

TUESDAY

SWIM

1

TIME/DISTANCE	COMMENTS

2

TIME/DISTANCE	COMMENTS

CYCLE

1

TIME/DISTANCE	COMMENTS

2

TIME/DISTANCE	COMMENTS

RUN

1

TIME/DISTANCE	COMMENTS

2

TIME/DISTANCE	COMMENTS

WEATHER CONDITIONS

HOW DO YOU FEEL

BEFORE TRAINING

AFTER TRAINING

WEDNESDAY

SWIM

1

TIME/DISTANCE	COMMENTS

2

TIME/DISTANCE	COMMENTS

CYCLE

1

TIME/DISTANCE	COMMENTS

2

TIME/DISTANCE	COMMENTS

RUN

1

TIME/DISTANCE	COMMENTS

2

TIME/DISTANCE	COMMENTS

WEATHER CONDITIONS

HOW DO YOU FEEL

BEFORE TRAINING

AFTER TRAINING

comments

THURSDAY

SWIM

1

TIME/DISTANCE	COMMENTS

2

TIME/DISTANCE	COMMENTS

CYCLE

1

TIME/DISTANCE	COMMENTS

2

TIME/DISTANCE	COMMENTS

RUN

1

TIME/DISTANCE	COMMENTS

2

TIME/DISTANCE	COMMENTS

WEATHER CONDITIONS

HOW DO YOU FEEL

BEFORE TRAINING

AFTER TRAINING

On your bike

Your bike needn't be expensive, but it must be reliable, and you should make sure that you train on the bike you will use in the race. Don't spend months training on one bike, then use an unfamiliar bike for the race.

Sea and lake training

Open-water swimming is very different from pool swimming; it requires a more upright position. You will also need to get used to the extra buoyancy that a wetsuit provides; this will also have an effect on your swimming position.

comments

FRIDAY

SWIM

1

TIME/DISTANCE	COMMENTS

2

TIME/DISTANCE	COMMENTS

CYCLE

1

TIME/DISTANCE	COMMENTS

2

TIME/DISTANCE	COMMENTS

RUN

1

TIME/DISTANCE	COMMENTS

2

TIME/DISTANCE	COMMENTS

WEATHER CONDITIONS

HOW DO YOU FEEL
BEFORE TRAINING

AFTER TRAINING

SATURDAY

SWIM

1

TIME/DISTANCE	COMMENTS

2

TIME/DISTANCE	COMMENTS

CYCLE

1

TIME/DISTANCE	COMMENTS

2

TIME/DISTANCE	COMMENTS

RUN

1

TIME/DISTANCE	COMMENTS

2

TIME/DISTANCE	COMMENTS

WEATHER CONDITIONS

HOW DO YOU FEEL
BEFORE TRAINING

AFTER TRAINING

SUNDAY

SWIM

1

TIME/DISTANCE	COMMENTS

2

TIME/DISTANCE	COMMENTS

CYCLE

1

TIME/DISTANCE	COMMENTS

2

TIME/DISTANCE	COMMENTS

RUN

1

TIME/DISTANCE	COMMENTS

2

TIME/DISTANCE	COMMENTS

WEATHER CONDITIONS

HOW DO YOU FEEL
BEFORE TRAINING

AFTER TRAINING

comments

DATE

GOALS MET

GOALS EXCEEDED

NEXT WEEK

SWIMMING NOTES

CYCLING NOTES

RUNNING NOTES

REFUELING NOTES

race-day preparation

Ultimately, triathlon is all about racing. It's about building your fitness in preparation for—at most—a handful of target events. And so it's vital you get your race day right. With that in mind, here are some race-day tips to help you make the most of your big day:

RELAX

Try to spend as little time on your feet as possible on the two days leading up to your race. Do your last-minute training sessions before lunchtime on the day before the race, then just relax. The chores can wait.

EAT TO PLAN

Don't eat anything the day before or the day of a race that you haven't tested in your training. Set the times you're going to eat, take your food and race nutrition with you to the race venue, and don't be tempted to try any of the freebies at the prerace expo. Save them for after you cross the finish line.

BE PREPARED

Pack all your race kit the day before the race. Work through a checklist (like the one on page 34), right down to filling your drink bottles, and then simply pick up the bags on race morning and head out to do battle.

GET THERE EARLY

Always aim to get to the race venue at least two hours before the start. That way, you'll have time to register, rack your bike, set out your kit, go to the bathroom, warm up, and change kit without any panicked rushing.

KNOW THE COURSE

If you can, train on the course at least once in the final weeks before the race. At least, figure out what the bike and run terrain and routes will be like, and then plan some training routes over similar terrain near where you live.

PLAN THE SWIM

If you're racing in open water, study the course from the shore with your swim course map in hand. Figure out where you turn, watch the current, and look for prominent landmarks to use as additional markers to keep you on course.

SET YOURSELF UP

Lay out your kit in a manner that suits you. For example: put down a towel beside your bike, place your run shoes in the middle, your bike shoes on either side of them, and your helmet on top of your shoes with the strap open. Check that your tires are pumped, your chain is oiled, your brakes aren't rubbing, and that your (full) drink bottle is on your bike.

WALK TRANSITION

Walk through the transition area noting the route from where you finish the swim to your bike, from where your bike is to the exit, and, finally, from where you re-enter transition after the bike leg, and out toward the start of the run. Recite in your head the things you must remember to do ("unzip wetsuit," "bike helmet fastened before grabbing bike," "run to bike exit, then mount up," "rerack bike before removing helmet," and so on).

WARM UP WELL

About 30 minutes before the race is due to start, head off for a 10-minute warm-up jog followed by a few 10-second race-pace accelerations. Then change into your race kit, head to the swim start, and finish your warm up in the water, practicing your start a couple of times and getting used to the water.

FOCUS AND RELAX

Consider taking an MP3 player and headphones to the race so that you can block out the rest of the world with some of your favorite, upbeat tunes.

glossary

Age Grouper–A nonelite, nonprofessional triathlete.

Aquathlon–A multisport race made up of a swim followed by a run.

BOP, FOP, MOP – Back Of the Packer, Front Of the Packer, Middle Of the Packer. How some triathletes (and runners) refer to themselves based on where they tend to finish in races.

Bottom bracket – The bearing and spindle to which the cranks are attached.

Brick – A training session combining two of the three triathlon disciplines in a continuous session, switching from one to the other and possibly back (e.g., bike/run/bike/run).

Cadence – The speed at which you turn the pedals around.

Cassette – The cluster of small gears attached to the rear wheel.

Chain-rings – The large gears attached to the bottom bracket and cranks.

Cleats – Plastic plates that you attach to the soles of your cycling shoes to clip them into clipless pedals.

Cranks – The metal arms to which the pedals are attached.

Derailleur (front and rear) – Spring-loaded mechanisms for changing gear. The front derailleur for the large chain wheels near the pedals, the rear derailleur for the cassette on the back wheel.

DNF, DNS – Did Not Finish and Did Not Start (on race results).

Drafting – Hiding behind another athlete during training or racing to conserve energy. Usually against the rules during the bike leg of a race, but acceptable during the swim leg (though often frowned upon during swim training).

Dropouts – The notches in the bike frame into which the wheels are secured.

Duathlon – A running and cycling only multisport race. Usually with the format run-bike-run.

Freewheel – The mechanism that allows your rear wheel to continue turning when you stop pedaling, or the act of not pedaling while on the road (usually down long or steep hills for recovery).

Front forks – The two blades that connect the front wheel to the rest of the bike.

ITU – International Triathlon Union. The world governing body of "Olympic" triathlon.

Mashing – Riding in a big gear at a low cadence. Sometimes also called grinding.

Negative split – Taking less time to complete the second half of a race, training session, or particular leg of a triathlon than you took to do the first half.

Quick-release skewers – The lever-tightened pins that thread through the hubs of your wheels and secure them in the dropouts.

Single-speed – A bicycle with only one gear but with a freewheel.

Spinning – Riding with a high cadence (often associated with easy recovery rides, warm-ups, and cool-downs).

Split – The time taken to complete a particular discipline during a triathlon (e.g., "bike split").

Sprockets – The individual small cogs that make up a cassette.

T1 – The transition from swim to bike.

T2 – The transition from bike to run.

Transition – Either the process of switching equipment and clothing between disciplines in a race, or the area (usually open only to competitors) in which those changes are made and where your equipment is stored.

Wave – A group of competitors in a staggered race who share the same start time. Often organized by age and gender.

WTC – World Triathlon Council. The governing body of Ironman-branded long-distance racing.

index

ACKNOWLEDGMENTS

Special thanks to Cannondale (*www.cannondale.com*), Asics (*www.asics.com*), Saucony (*www.saucony.com*), and Polar (*www.polarusa.com*) for their help with equipment and images.

We apologize in advance for any unintentional credit omissions. We would be pleased to insert the appropriate acknowledgment in any subsequent edition of this publication.